Praise for

and Shine in Law School with Gratitude, Grit, and Grace

"Good news at last for law students grappling with all the things that law school brings! *How to Show Up and Shine in Law School* reminds us that our strength lies in our origin stories, and that we can use the skills we are developing as lawyers, to be creative problem solvers, to solve the multiple 'tests' we face as students and eventual practitioners. Bravo to Cherelle for sharing common sense tools for success in plain English. I wish I had this guide when I was a 1L long ago; it sends a clear message to all, especially women and underrepresented folks, that from the moment of acceptance to law school, you belong."

—Tomasita Sherer, Partner Dentons

"How to Show up and Shine in Law School with Gratitude, Grit, and Grace is a beacon of wisdom and encouragement for anyone embarking on their law school journey. This book is a guide for aspiring lawyers full of invaluable insights and a refreshing perspective on the challenges law students face. It's not just about the legal intricacies; it's also about staying grounded, mindful, and connected to one's purpose, which are qualities that can often be overshadowed by the rigors of law school."

—Nicole Lester Arrindell, Esq. President, Metropolitan Black Bar Association

"In the realm of law school, where the path is often arduous and filled with challenges, *How to Show up and Shine in Law School with Gratitude, Grit, and Grace* stands out as a beacon of guidance and inspiration. It is my firm belief that this book should be a mandatory gift to all aspiring law students upon their registration and acceptance into university.

From the very first page, this book captivates the reader with its practical wisdom, sage advice, subtle humor, and a treasure trove of strategies and tips for not just surviving but thriving in the demanding world of law school. As someone who has been practicing law for 27 years and mentoring countless law students, I can confidently say that this book is a game-changer.

What truly sets this book apart is its thoughtful structure. At the end of each chapter, the author includes a set of questions that serve as a reset button, gently nudging the reader to reflect on the invaluable lessons just learned. This ingenious feature not only encourages self-assessment but also provides a moment of pause and introspection, which is often overlooked in the whirlwind of legal studies.

Throughout my reading journey, I found myself reaching for post-it notes, a highlighter, and even folding pages to ensure I could return to the profound insights within. The book's pages are now adorned with my personal annotations, a testament to its enduring relevance and the wealth of knowledge it imparts.

The author's ability to combine practical advice with a touch of humor is a refreshing and effective approach.

In conclusion, this book transcends the boundaries of a mere guidebook; it is a mentor, a friend, and a confidant for anyone embarking on the challenging journey of law school. I wholeheartedly recommend it to all law students, both aspiring and current, as well as to seasoned legal professionals who could benefit from a dose of rejuvenation and wisdom.

Kudos to the author for a job exceedingly well done!"

—Nicolle Kopping-Pavars, author; former family law lawyer; certified mindfulness instructor; trauma awareness activist, success coach.

"This important book has the potential to transform the law school experience for countless law students—shifting the focus from surviving to thriving. With humor and a healthy dose of insight drawn from thought leaders, influential psychological research and personal stories of her own law school experience, Cherelle sets forth a thoughtful and actionable roadmap to skillfully navigate many of law school's most common and challenging hurdles. Poignant reminders of belonging, worthiness, and the power of gratitude are reinforced throughout the book offering readers the inner tools for not only finding fulfillment in the study and practice of law but for a lifelong journey of personal growth and wellbeing."

—Scott L. Rogers, M.S., J.D., Director, Mindfulness in Law Program University of Miami School of Law, author of *The Mindful Law Student: A Mindfulness in Law Practice Guide*

"*How to Show Up and Shine in Law School with Gratitude, Grit, and Grace* is a thought-provoking and valuable book that offers a distinctive perspective on excelling in law school. Its focus on character development, professionalism, and self-care is a testament to the holistic approach needed in legal education. This is a must-read for any law student or lawyer who wants to develop a positive mindset and build resilience as they journey through their career."

—Karen Munoz, Partner-Dolan Law / Wellness Advocate

"This compassionate, informative, and highly practical book will give students the necessary skills to excel in law school. This should be required reading."

—Gary Linnen, CEO PeerForward

"Cherelle's book, *How to Show Up and Shine in Law School with Gratitude, Grit and Grace*, is a powerful source of inspiration for 1L students, reminding them that the same courage, determination, and resilience that brought them to law school will not only enable their success but empower them to blaze their own trail in their legal journey. Cherelle eloquently exhibits how gratitude, the support of a personal affirmation committee, embracing stretch opportunities, and practicing kindness serve as indispensable tools for not merely surviving but thriving in law school. She provides invaluable guidance on overcoming imposter syndrome, shedding the burden of perfectionism, and sidestepping the pitfalls of comparison. Cherelle offers no-nonsense mentorship to 1L students, equipping them with insights into mastering the Socratic method, excelling in exam preparation, and "thinking like a lawyer." Her work is a true gift not only to 1Ls but indeed to the legal profession, leaving an indelible mark on those who embrace her wisdom."

—Carrie Rodarte, US/UK qualified lawyer, professional executive and health and wellness coach for lawyers, Red Tree Coaching, LL

"*How to Show Up and Shine in Law School* is a compilation of very useful practical tips for keeping one's eye on the goal of doing well in law school while enjoying life and being grateful for one's place in this new world of legal education. It explains how to set up good support systems, avoid negative thinking, learn legal education techniques, have meaningful conversations and speak truth to power, and achieve one's goals using the best techniques from positive psychology and mindfulness practices. It is a book I would recommend to my students."

—Nathalie Martin, Frederick M. Hart Chair in Consumer and Clinical Law, University of New Mexico School of Law, author of Lawyering from the Inside

"Cherelle provides actionable tools for law students to implement. If they do so, I'm confident they'll succeed, just as she hopes they will. What is most compelling about this book is that the tips aren't just for law students. The tools Cherelle provides would help the most senior attorneys refresh and reset their practices. Cherelle's vulnerability to share her own story, which, like most of us, includes some hiccups, creates credibility. She sets out intentional practices that will help law students find contentment and fulfillment during a typically trying time. Cherelle offers a playbook for law students to differentiate themselves and thrive. Law students that find, read, and implement these techniques will have a leg up as they enter the profession."

—Emily Logan Stedman, Senior Associate, Husch Blackwell, State Bar of Wisconsin, Young Lawyers Division, Past President; Wisconsin Taskforce on Lawyer Well-Being, Inaugural Member and Committee Chair, 2020-2022

"This book is a valuable resource for underrepresented, current and prospective law students. The book provides insightful strategies and guidance on how to navigate law school using a self-awareness and intentional approach. The book provides insight into the law school experience while embracing mindfulness techniques. The book's emphasis on self-awareness, identity, and resilience offers a fresh perspective. The inclusion of real-life examples enhances uniqueness and authenticity. Overall, it is a highly recommended read for those seeking to excel in their law school journey. In sum, *How to Show up and Shine in Law School with Gratitude, Grit, and Grace* is a must-read for anyone embarking on the path to legal education."

—De'Jonique Carter, Esq., Pre-Law Advisor Dillard University School of Law

"I wish I had *How to Show Up and Shine in Law School with Gratitude, Grit, and Grace* as a resource for me, a child of immigrants, when I decided to go to law school and had absolutely no idea what I was getting myself into. With excellent, new-age advice on how to succeed in law school and deal with imposter syndrome, this book is a must read for every incoming law student, but especially for those who do not have mentors or resources to help them navigate through law school. Cherelle is exactly the advocate, guidance counselor, mentor, and author the legal community needs."

—Tina Lapsia, Associate Manatt, Phelps & Phillips, LLP

"In this law school prep book, Cherelle shares her experience and wisdom learned through years of practice (along with her share of suffering, to be sure), so that students might experience a bit more peace, love, and joy along their path. Make no mistake, law school and the legal profession can be demanding. But you got this. And this book can help."

—Joseph Milowic III, Director of Well-Being & Of Counsel at Quinn Emanuel Urquhart & Sullivan, LLP and Co-Founder of the Lawyers Depression Project (www.lawyersdepressionproject.org), a non-profit which provides an online peer support community for legal professionals (not just lawyers).

"When I started law school, I lost some of the people I relied on most for emotional support. For example, my mother died the day before my first law school final. While that sounds like an extreme and unusual situation (and it is —law school will not kill your mom), the surprising thing to me was not the death of my mom, which was expected, but instead the fact that life went on while I was having the most intense academic experience of my life. I did not have the tools at the time to process the losses I was experiencing and the confrontation with my own inadequacies that law school challenged me to make, so I just compartmentalized the best I could, vented about petty issues to my friends, and tried to survive.

At the time, I remember staring at the bookshelf in my school's Career Services office, flipping through books, thinking, "Where is the book that will tell me I might be able to be good at something? How will I know if I am ever good at something?" And, mind you, I was someone who did well in law school and appreciated the academic challenge, so I had very clear privilege. *How to Show up and Shine in Law School* is the book I didn't know I needed at the time. This book has practical, step-by-step, straightforward guidance about how to personally not just survive, but succeed, while you are academically torn down and built up again by the law school process.

This week, I had a 1L tell me she just wanted to know the "blueprint" for success in law school. I told her it was IRAC/CREAC, which this book also highlights, but much more than that, the blueprint for success in law school is each of the steps this book goes through. Know how to replenish yourself and not just drain yourself; make plans for how you want to show up when you encounter discrimination and abuse; give your closest people copies of this book so they can effectively support you.

Anyone who has graduated from law school in the past twenty years, maybe more, has probably debated the value of a law degree or whether it is impossible to really "make a difference." This book is a practical how-to guide for making your law degree valuable so that you can make a difference."

—Meredith Holley, communication coach, workplace conflict mediator, civil rights attorney, author of *Career Defense 101: How to Stop Sexual Harassment Without Quitting Your Job*; author of *The Inclusive Leader's Guide to Healthy Workplace Culture*

"Cherelle's book will be an outstanding resource for law students—her kind, optimistic, and supportive voice resound throughout and reflect precisely the wonderful law school classmate she was to me in law school. Law school can be a daunting experience full of many ups and downs, but Cherelle's book demonstrates that you can take practicable steps to mastering the experience, starting with embracing that you fully belong. Cherelle shares her experiences to provide practical advice about how to battle imposter syndrome; feel gratitude even in challenging moments; speak your truth; and how to exercise self-care so you can guard your energy and focus. This will be a wonderful gift to new law school students—bravo to Cherelle!"

—Mia Martin, law school classmate and in-house lawyer.

"In *How to Show Up and Shine in Law School with Gratitude, Grit and Grace*, Cherelle masterfully guides readers through the intricacies of law student awareness. This book isn't just another self-help manual; it's a transformative experience that offers Cherelle's perspective from being accepted to resisting mediocrity. Cherelle's wisdom and understanding of 'mindful redirection'—her strategy to show and make your presence known with elegance' are unparalleled. I was particularly moved by her cross-examination of unproductive thoughts and framework for maximizing goals. I enthusiastically recommend this book to anyone looking to begin their legal career and deepen their understanding of holistic well-being and balance. It is truly life-changing work she shares with her readers."

—Michele Adler, holistic coach, LMT, FS

"For over three decades, I have learned, developed, and coached my specialized programs that help people protect and preserve their greatest assets (brain and body) in order to thrive personally and professionally. For the last several years, my clients are mostly lawyers, from first year associates to senior partners in top global law firms. Lawyers come to me when they realize that they have given up parts of themselves, gotten into self-harming habits, and/or feel as though they lost years of their lives and important opportunities. In every case, if they had this book in law school they would likely need me a whole lot less!

Cherelle intuitively presents essential concepts for law students that will undoubtedly save their mental and physical wellness from the grueling demands and expectations. *How to Show Up and Shine in Law School with Gratitude, Grit, and Grace* is a manual for how to be a whole human in law school. Cherelle emphasizes self-care as a daily practice and the secret sauce for a successful life as a lawyer. My hope is that the next generation of lawyers develops a strong sense of quality life balancing and shapes the culture of law firms with a human-centered approach."

—Ava Diamond, LCSW, brain & body optimization coaching, certified in nutritional psychiatry and brain health

"Cherelle's book should be required reading for all 1Ls, not just those who identify as diverse! Cherelle brilliantly blends providing her readers with practical tips for how to survive and thrive in law school (e.g., how to 'take control of the Socratic Method by Being Prepared') with practical and manageable self-care tips such as those found in each chapter's Concluding Mindfulness Practice. A lot of us who attend law school are over-achievers who weren't prepared for the first year of law school nor the actual practice of law. Coming from someone who burned out as a lawyer, Cherelle's approachable style would have been helpful to me as a 1L and as a new practicing attorney. In fact, even as a registered yoga teacher and licensed (but not practicing) attorney today, Cherelle provides many new take-aways for those of us who are many years beyond law school to apply to our lives and our practices. Thank you, Cherelle, for showing up and shining—and sharing with us your gratitude, grit, and grace!"

—Kitty Wetherington, attorney, HR professional, yoga alliance registered yoga teacher 200 (RYT200), wellness educator, and North Carolina DRC certified mediator

"Cherelle's book is the type of resource I wish existed when I was in law school. Using an optimistic and encouraging tone, Cherelle not only imparts invaluable insights into the rigors of law school but also arms the reader with pragmatic, actionable strategies. With a clear understanding of what it takes to succeed in law school, Cherelle gives relevant examples and soothing guidance that make you feel like you truly can enjoy the experience. It's not merely a guide; it's a compass, leading you not just through the intricacies of legal education but toward a fulfilling and enjoyable journey in the realm of law. As a prelaw advisor at a large university, I highly encourage anyone interested in going to law school to pick up this book!"

—Gabriela Brunner, JD, MS, Pre-Law Advisor at the University of Illinois at Urbana-Champaign

"*How To Show Up and Shine in Law School with Gratitude, Grit, and Grace* is the must-have primer for anyone thinking about or starting law school. It is a wealth of practical information for navigating the experiences of 1L life. Cherelle is honest about the challenges of being a 1L, but also provides incredible strategies and tips for maximizing one's law school experience so that law school can be a catapulting experience for one's legal career."

—Alyssa Johnson, Esq., CLE instructor, coach and consultant

HOW TO SHOW UP AND SHINE IN LAW SCHOOL WITH GRATITUDE, GRIT, AND GRACE

Cherelle Iman Glimp

Pact Press

Published by Fitzroy Books
An imprint of
Regal House Publishing, LLC
Raleigh, NC 27605
All rights reserved

https://fitzroybooks.com
Printed in the United States of America

ISBN -13 (paperback): 9781646035236
ISBN -13 (epub): 9781646035243
Library of Congress Control Number: TBD

All efforts were made to determine the copyright holders and obtain their permissions in any circumstance where copyrighted material was used. The publisher apologizes if any errors were made during this process, or if any omissions occurred. If noted, please contact the publisher and all efforts will be made to incorporate permissions in future editions.

Cover images and design by

Regal House Publishing, LLC
https://regalhousepublishing.com

Printed in the United States of America

To my family, including my beloved parents.

Mom, dad, you are my guiding light, my pillar of strength, and the ultimate form of unconditional love.

Thank you for showing up for me and instilling the message: *With God, all things are possible.*

Contents

Introduction

The Admissions Committee Has Handpicked YOU

If you weren't capable, the opportunity would have never come your way. You belong.

—Sukari A. Brown, PMP

The word "CONGRATULATIONS" levitated off the page. It was the only word that mattered as I nervously ripped open the long-awaited letter from Columbia Law School. Everything else on the page blurred into the empty white space. When I received the life-changing news that I had been accepted, I remember exactly where I was, who was nearby, and the first person I called to share the exciting announcement. It was no longer theoretical. I had an acceptance letter in my hand, with my name on it, welcoming me to the incoming class of law students. In that moment, I proudly became a "1L."

Beginnings are incredibly special. The thrill of new adventures can also evoke unease, especially for soon-to-be law students. If you can relate, don't panic! Trust me, you *are* ready for the exciting journey ahead.

You have been chosen, hand selected, in fact, for this once-in-a-lifetime period of intense study and self-discovery. Luck had nothing to do with your acceptance into law school. You were not admitted because of your connections (although I'm sure you have influential movers and shakers in your network). It was not because the stars cosmically aligned. You have earned this opportunity, so celebrate the sacrifices and willpower that ushered you to this point. Give yourself credit for what you have already accomplished.

Law school is a unique academic and professional pursuit. It is a momentous opportunity to analyze legal doctrines and grapple with controversial issues that impact healthcare, criminal justice, environmental policy, housing, education, employment, and many other systems that demand thoughtful attention, now more than ever. Think about it this way. Individuals and corporations typically do not seek legal advice when the pieces of the puzzle seamlessly fit together. Instead, cries for help and alarm bells sound when the business failed, the marriage crumbled, someone unfairly lost their job, or some other injustice has occurred. You are entering a helping profession, which means you will aid people and companies when they need legal expertise. In these moments of desperation, your future clients will hire you—a cutting-edge thinker and problem solver to step in. The legal profession needs *you*.

Law school will stretch you in new and uncomfortable ways. (If you thought that yoga class turned you into a pretzel, wait until your first semester as a 1L.) This experience will recalibrate your intellectual stamina, sharpen your perspectives, and even test beliefs you once thought were unshakeable. Buckle up!

More than a decade ago, I *thought* I was ready to start law school. Everything was seemingly in order—the LSAT was thankfully a distant memory, those who knew my story had graciously reviewed every iteration of my personal statement, and the Law School Admission Council received my letters of recommendation. I can't remember how many times I scrutinized my application materials, agonizing over every detail. My Type A readers know what I'm talking about. Then came the hard part: holding my breath, waiting to hear "Congratulations," "We regret to inform you," or the law school equivalent of "It's complicated" (i.e., "You've been waitlisted").

While I knew I wanted to attend law school, I had no

clue what to actually expect, other than spending endless hours hunkered over massive case books in the library. I also ignored important threshold questions law students should honestly consider. Starting with the basics, I didn't know why I wanted to be a lawyer or how I planned to use my law degree. I had generic, unimaginative answers like "I want to make a difference and help people in some way," and "I want to be challenged intellectually." But beyond this, was my decision to attend law school driven by the allure of a lucrative career? Stability? The pride in telling people, while humble bragging, that "I'm a lawyer" when asked what I do for a living?

Before law school, there were many unanswered questions that I didn't even know needed consideration. How would I respond to fear? Disappointment? Setbacks? Worry? Burnout? Stress? Feelings of "imposterism"? Overwhelm? Exhaustion? Anxiety? Isolation? What if I didn't measure up to my own definition of success (or the definitions others imposed)? I'll put it this way—many of my law school "tests" were not on the syllabus. The same may be true for you.

Without thoughtfully reflecting on these questions, when challenges arose in law school, I would often wonder, "What in the world have I gotten myself into?" I needed assurances that mistakes were part of the process and that my self-worth was not externally defined—not by an exam grade or performing well during a Socratic session (more about that later). I craved reminders to be patient with myself and not jump to unfounded conclusions when challenges unexpectedly emerged.

If no one soothes your law school-related anxieties, that's okay. Hear it from me. You are in the right place at the right time with the right tools to blaze a trail that will make you proud. You are ready for what lies ahead, despite what you may feel.

You've heard the phrase "bought as is," right? Well, the

admissions committee has accepted you "as is." Law schools are a business, after all, and their financial model would collapse if they haphazardly admitted students with little prospect of graduating, securing gainful employment, or becoming meaningful contributors as alumni. My point is, you don't need to do anything else to qualify for your seat. You have already earned it. It's yours. Own it. Be expansive. Add value. Be radiant. Contribute. No one can say it with your voice, inflection, tone, conviction, accent, cadence, or expression, so if *you* do not speak, it won't be said. Although law school will thrust you into an environment where everyone is academically talented, you too belong in this league of brilliance, just as you are, right now.

As you embark on your legal quest, this book will cheer you on by emphasizing belonging, worthiness, and gratitude. It will help you show up and shine. Merely surviving law school is not energizing or impactful. Aiming to just "get by" preserves the status quo. Law school is a golden opportunity to forge relationships with your peers, professors, guest speakers, legal practitioners, career advisors, and alumni. Starting today, begin nurturing these relationships. Law school is the time to say "yes" to opportunities, even if you don't feel ready. At graduation, I want you to proudly sashay across the stage, knowing that you squeezed the last drop out of every opportunity law school presents.

Survival is important. Thriving is elegant.

—Maya Angelou

In this book, I'll share what I wish I'd known before becoming a 1L, starting with feelings of "imposter syndrome." Chapter 1 tackles this phenomenon and provides strategies to minimize feeling like a fraud. Chapter 2 describes gratitude as an excellent coping mechanism and an important anxiety antidote for law students and legal practitioners. Are you familiar with the African proverb "it takes a village to raise a child"? This saying reminds us that a child's upbringing is a communal effort that extends beyond one's immediate family. What about the law student's "village" of supporters? Chapter 3 provides conversation starters and insight into how your community can show up for you over the next three years.

If you are concerned about final exams and managing the Socratic method (or don't even know what that is), chapter 4 prepares you for these challenges. In chapter 4, you will learn to focus on what you can control as a law student and identify the "controllables" in every situation.

As a lawyer in training, get ready to speak truth to power, whether on your own behalf or as an advocate for others. The way you approach these conversations can determine your success. How can you speak up in a way that invites curiosity, not confrontation? In those uncomfortable, uneasy conversations, how can you boldly say what needs to be said and feel empowered while doing so? Chapter 5 introduces the concept of "mindful redirection," using pointed verbal responses to gain clarity, diffuse tension, and speak up in the moment.

Feeling the urge to compare yourself to the student who *says* they spent fifteen hours preparing for class? It's a trap; don't fall for it! Chapter 6 cautions against comparing yourself to other law students; this is a distraction that can siphon away valuable resources—your time, energy, and motivation. Chapter 7 invites you to cross-examine negative, unproductive thoughts that can stonewall opportunities within reach during law school and beyond. With the tools described in chapter 7, you will be equipped to redirect negative thoughts to make bold moves toward your future.

Chapter 8 debunks the myth that you need to multitask to #GetThingsDone and encourages you to be intentional with your time. Finally, chapter 9 gives you the tools to transcend mediocrity in law school.

This three-year journey is the time to go all in. It's the time to take risks and fully show up to every class, conversation, and event with gusto. You can do more than "get by." Instead, invite curiosity into your law school experience and courageously try new things, recognizing that you can create your own plot twist at any time. Each chapter concludes with a short mindfulness exercise that you can incorporate into your law school routine and reflection questions to help you uncover ways to lighten the path ahead.

Let me be clear: hacks, short cuts, or magic formulas to flourish in law school do not exist. Yes, we know excelling in this profession takes effort, but it also requires perspective, self-regulation, and daily reminders to give yourself grace. We will explore these concepts and more.

After reading this book, you will have a game-changing guide to succeed in law school. Before we dive in, several disclaimers are in order (I'm a lawyer, so I can't help it). First, I am not a therapist, so please seek professional guidance if the law school daily grind starts to negatively impact your mental, physical, or emotional health. There are on-campus resources, some of which may be free, that can help you develop positive coping mechanisms that are tailored to your specific needs. Second, my goal is not to assume that your law school journey will resemble mine. Everyone's experience is different. And importantly, everyone's experience is what they make it. The pages that follow reflect the best advice *I* have to offer. Finally, everything I share in this book is an invitation. So, if the recommendations do not resonate with you, I won't be offended if you don't RSVP to the advice-giving party.

With this guide, I am accepting the late author Toni Morrison's challenge: "If there's a book that you want to read, but it hasn't been written yet, then you must write it." This is my book.

1

Think, Act, and Be Expansive—Even If You Feel Like an Imposter

Imposter syndrome will have you questioning your place in the spaces that you prayed about being in. It's a lie. You're capable. You're allowed to learn. You belong.

—Jonathan Pulliam II

"Congratulations," reads your acceptance letter. "We are delighted to welcome you to our incoming class of law students. Among the thousands of applications we received this year, the Admissions Committee intentionally selected you based on your academic record and commitment to excellence. By admitting you to this school, the Admissions Committee firmly believes that you will contribute to our community, the legal profession, and beyond. We are excited about what the future holds for you."

I'm not a high-maintenance author, and I promise not to overwhelm you with an unreasonable number of "asks" throughout this book. But I will make several requests along the way to make the recommendations personal and immediately actionable. The first ask is an important one.

Ask #1: Dust off your law school acceptance letter!

If your acceptance letter is in your email inbox, track it down and print it out. If it's posted online, bookmark the page. If you have a hard copy, scan it, or take a picture of the letter just in case you misplace the original. Make it the home screen on your laptop and cell phone. Okay, you get the point. Your acceptance letter is a prized possession to hold close during your law school journey.

Why? This letter, with your name on it, addressed specifically to you, is undeniable and empirical proof that you have earned the right to proudly occupy every nook, cranny, and crevice of the law school experience. All of it. Your acceptance letter is a tangible reminder that the admissions committee made the right decision saying "yes" to you. Full stop; no qualification needed.

Have you ever wondered why lawyers and other professionals proudly display their degrees in their offices? This is a visual reminder that they have earned their seat, even if they experience an occasional twinge of self-doubt. So, when you get your first job after law school, keep your employment agreement or offer letter close by as proof of belonging.

What Is Imposter Syndrome?

In this chapter, we will explore what imposter syndrome is and discuss actionable strategies to minimize the feeling when it arises.

The term "imposter syndrome" isn't new. It was coined in 1978 by psychologists Pauline Rose Clance and Suzanne Imes. They defined imposter syndrome as feeling inadequate despite evidence to the contrary.[1] Clance and Imes elaborated as follows:

> [D]espite their earned degrees, scholastic honors, high achievement on standardized tests, praise and professional recognition from colleagues and respected authorities, these women do not experience an internal sense of success. They consider themselves to be "imposters." Women who experience the imposter phenomenon maintain a strong belief that they are not intelligent; in fact, they are convinced that they have fooled anyone who thinks otherwise.[2]

---

[1] Pauline Rose Clance & Suzanne Ament Imes, *The Imposter Phenomenon in High Achieving Women: Dynamics and Therapeutic Intervention*, Psychotherapy: Theory, Research and Practice, vol. 15, no. 3 (1978).
[2] *Id.*

Although Clance and Imes initially studied imposter syndrome as a phenomenon that only impacted women, we now understand that it can affect anyone, including people who *seem* like they have it all together. By using the word "syndrome," Clance and Imes did not intend to diagnose women with a pathology. Instead, they wanted to normalize a specific experience the women in their study described. Going forward, I will not refer to this phenomenon as a "syndrome" because that could imply a mental or emotional abnormality that needs medical intervention. When I use the term in this book, my intent is to describe sentiments of self-doubt, fear of not meeting expectations, and feeling inadequate.

Feelings of "imposterism" may intensify in law school because nearly *everything* will be unfamiliar: a new academic environment, a new cast of characters, new routines, new structures, new challenges, and even a new language. In no time, Latin phrases like *sua sponte, prima facie, in camera, mens rea,* and *quantum meruit* will roll off your tongue. But in the beginning, the newness of it all can be intimidating. Before reading any further, say this out loud: "I have never been a law student. Therefore, it is normal, no *expected,* that I will encounter new experiences. I have permission to be a beginner. I will allow myself to be a student."

The imposter phenomenon can manifest itself in many ways. Surrounded by novelty at every turn, students may feel like an intruder when interacting with other accomplished classmates, the crème de la crème from their respective colleges, or after being called on for the first time during a Socratic session. Students attending law school immediately after college may believe they are less credentialed compared to classmates who have established careers before assuming 1L status. Those who returned to school after a temporary hiatus may feel out of place relative to students who went straight to law school after college. International students may feel insecure about learning the law in a secondary language. If you have imposter-like moments, you are not alone.

Unanswered Questions Do Not Make You An Imposter

You *will* have unanswered questions before starting law school. But this does not make you an imposter. You may be pondering some of the following:

- Do I have what it takes to meet the academic demands law school presents?
- What's the best way to prepare for law school?
- What if I don't know what specific area of the law interests me?
- How will I pay for my legal education?
- Should I participate in extracurricular activities? If so, which ones?
- Should I pursue Law Review or other writing opportunities? If so, how do I balance these activities with my course work and personal responsibilities?
- How should I select my elective courses? Should I take classes that will be tested on the bar exam? Or should I register for classes that genuinely interest me?
- Should I participate in a legal clinic to gain practical skills?
- Should I apply for a judicial clerkship, internship, or externship?
- Should I apply for a joint degree program such as a JD/MBA or a JD/Masters?
- Who makes up my law school support system?
- How will I communicate with my support system what I may need?
- What are my law school self-care practices?
- Who will hold me accountable when I don't prioritize self-care?
- Who will remind me of how capable I am if self-doubt arises?

You are not a phony simply because you have questions.

Deliberate investigation means you care about your future and want to make strategic decisions. Continue asking questions and know that it may take time to discover the answers. When you receive advice, yes, even the well-intentioned recommendations in this book, scrutinize what you hear and be intensely curious about everything. Savor the process of information gathering and be patient with yourself. If you knew the answer to every law school-related question today, there would be no soul-stirring epiphanies to experience over the next three years. In short, the more examining you are, the better prepared you will be to maximize your law school experience.

At times, I felt like an imposter when I walked to and from class and encountered looming portraits of my law school's alumni adorning the hallways and classrooms. Almost every day, I greeted esteemed images of judges, professors, civil servants, and legal practitioners. Most of the images were of white men. Yes, they were remarkable scholars and practitioners, but there was a noticeable lack of similarly distinguished women and attorneys of color featured in the hallways and lecture halls. Because I looked nothing like the people reflected in these portraits, I sometimes felt disqualified from learning in this space. It was as if the images whispered "outcast," "other," "imposter," or "trespasser" every time I walked by. Of course, the portraits seemed to cast their most confidence-deflating shadows on days when I already felt outmatched.

The images that induced feelings of inadequacy (or that I *allowed* to make me feel that way) were not the only representations of success. It was my job—and it may be yours—to assemble a collection of powerful images that unequivocally impart the message, "If I can do it, so can you." In *The Secret Thoughts of Successful Women: Why Capable People Suffer From Impostor Syndrome and How to Thrive in Spite of It*, Dr. Valerie

Young writes:

> Don't confuse the discomfort caused from feeling out-
> numbered with thinking you're not smart enough or are
> in some way not worthy of being there. You are where
> you are because you deserve to be. Being one of a to-
> ken few can be stressful. Which makes it all the more
> important that when impostor feelings do strike, you
> give yourself extra points for performing as well as you
> do. You may be expected to represent your entire social
> group, but you need not accept that responsibility. Assert
> your right to fall as flat on your face as the next person.[3]

You cannot be an imposter in your own home. Your acceptance letter has *your* name on it, remember? For the next
three years, law school is your new residence. So, make it
your own—get cozy. Settle in.

You are meant to be exactly where you are, despite the
imposter sensations you may experience. It's only a sensation
because you are not a fraud—you can uniquely impact any
classroom, courtroom, or conference room you enter. Your
admission to law school is no accident, and the fear of being
"discovered" as a fraud is only an illusion. Consider these
recommendations to help minimize feelings of imposterism
in law school and beyond.

Create An "Anti-Imposter List"

Law schools do not hand out acceptance letters without careful thought. You worked for that "yes" from the admissions
committee. Think back to the countless hours you spent toil-
ing over logic games and practicing reading comprehension
questions to prepare for the LSAT? Celebrate the academic
and professional achievements you have already attained.
These past victories prove that you know how to roll up your

[3] Valerie Young, *The Secret Thoughts of Successful Women and Men: Why Capable People Suffer From Impostor Syndrome and How to Thrive in Spite of It* (Currency: New York 2011) 44.

sleeves and get your hands dirty, if that's what the challenge requires. The discipline that led you to this point will continue propelling you forward. So, when the nagging "I-don't-know-if-I-can-do-this" attitude rears its ugly head, think like a lawyer, and dig into the facts, counselor-to-be. Your personal evidentiary record is filled with examples of you triumphing over challenges; law school will be no different.

To create your anti-imposter list, gather your academic achievements (transcripts, letters of recommendation, laudatory emails from college professors, anything you can get your hands on). Include your personal accomplishments too—important relationships you have nurtured over the years, examples of you showing up for friends, caring for family, or simply being a kind and decent citizen. You can also include experiences you have survived and ways in which you have navigated past obstacles. This list will look different for everyone. The goal is to identify all areas in which you have excelled so you can refer to this motivating set of data points.

Here's a bonus. With your anti-imposter list in hand, you can reverse engineer what contributed to your success. For example, what qualities or practices led to the achievements you have listed? Your persistence, patience, compassion? How can you activate those same qualities so they can work for you now?

Notice Your Thoughts

In law school, every day you will be expected to synthesize seemingly endless volumes of information. You do not have time to entertain false narratives that you do not belong. This is a distraction. If you allow thoughts of imposterism to linger, you may decline important "stretch" opportunities, fearing that you are not qualified or ready. But you are. And even if you are not ready at the time, trust that you will figure it out. The longer those thoughts loiter, the more likely patterns will develop around the myth that you are not "[blank]" enough (i.e., smart enough, creative enough, experienced enough). If you don't stop feelings of imposterism, this can also lead to burn out before you've had a bona fide chance to demonstrate how capable you truly are. There is much more to be said about noticing your thoughts, and chapter 7 provides practical strategies to help you recognize negative thought patterns that often involve cognitive distortions.

Recognize That You Are Learning How to Practice Law

Minimize imposterism sensations by recognizing that the legal profession is centered around practice. Is that relieving or what? We get to hone our skills over time through repetition and refinement. Lawyers in most states must participate in continuing legal education ("CLE") programs to maintain their license to practice law. From newly minted lawyers to senior practitioners, lawyers must continuously sharpen their skills by obtaining CLE credits every few years.

Practice is so rooted in the profession that lawyers are generally prohibited from using terms like "expert" and "specialist" when advertising their services to the public. For example, if an attorney wanted to promote their business by saying they are an "expert" in bankruptcy law, this could lead to ethical or disciplinary issues. Although the rules of professional conduct are state specific, the American Bar Association publishes model guidelines that restrict lawyers from stating that they are "certified as a specialist in a particular field" unless they have actually been trained by an accredited organization, authorized by their state.

Practice Means Prioritizing The Process, Not The Prize

Success follows the grind you love.

—Felicia Day, author of *Embrace Your Weird*

Practice is focused on the process—the side of the equation you can control. It often consists of behind the scenes work that leads to the final product. I would imagine that award-winning vocalists relish the steps that lead to performing for sold-out concerts. Artists at the top of their craft enjoy rehearsals, practicing scales, composing music, recording albums, or listening to other musicians. They may even find joy in the process, regardless of the outcome. Think about it this way. What kind of performance would a professional singer deliver if they were reluctant to engage wholeheartedly in the process? A best-in-class performance is only possible with best-in-class practice.

How does this apply to lawyers? Let's say you are part of a litigation team, preparing for a jury trial. Of course, the goal is to convince a group of strangers that your client should win—that's the desired outcome. To get to the ultimate win, your partner asks you to research an evidentiary issue and draft a motion to exclude harmful evidence. Being process-oriented means finding the best cases (sometimes the needle in the haystack), taking your time to explore the nuances of the rules, the exceptions to the rules, the weight of authority, cases your adversary may cite to refute your position, and how you would respond to those arguments. The desire to win the jury trial means nothing if you are not willing to prioritize the seemingly unimportant steps along the way. In many ways, the process determines the outcome.

Mathematician Paul Halmos sums it up this way: "[T]he true mark of a pro—at anything—is that he understands, loves, and is good at even the drudgery of his profession."

While in law school and as you embark on your legal career, discover parts of the process you enjoy. You are not going to land every client that you pitch. Deals fall through. You certainly will not win every litigation or arbitration. There will be times when you walk away from a mediation feeling like you have given up more than you are getting in return. Conditioning our sense of fulfillment on outcomes alone negates the value and excitement of the process itself. As lawyers, if we consistently find ourselves avoiding, suffering through, or dreading our processes, it may be time to pause and reassess.

James Clear, author of *Atomic Habits*, encourages us to fall in love with systems (i.e., practice), rather than outcomes. Clear writes:

> A systems-first mentality provides the antidote. When you fall in love with the process rather than the product, you don't have to wait to give yourself permission to be happy. You can be satisfied anytime your system is running. And a system can be successful in many different forms, not just the one you first envision.[4]

My hope is that you will identify parts of the law school process that get you in a state of flow, where you feel fulfilled, regardless of the outcome. If you don't enjoy the process and the systems that contribute to what you are doing, it may be time to reorient yourself toward something that leads to more fluidity.

Practice And Feedback Work Hand-in-Hand

Practice and feedback have a symbiotic relationship. Think about the best athletes in the world and those who contribute to their success. Athletic coaches spot weaknesses and amplify strengths by saying things like "take your time," "push harder," "keep going," "run faster," "one play/game/match/meet/race at a time," "go higher," "breathe through it," "get back up," and "do it again" (even if the athlete perfectly nailed the drill). During practice, athletes learn how to remain composed through the exhaustion and pressure. When game day comes, they can perform at a high level because of the habits they developed during practice.

There is no shame in relying on someone to usher you closer to your best. Your law school professors, mentors, advisors, and alumni are your professional coaches, who can remind you that you are not an imposter.

[4] James Clear, *Atomic Habits: An Easy & Proven Way to Build Good Habits & Break Bad Ones* (New York: Avery, 2018) 26.

Because The Law Is Dynamic, You Will Always Be A Student

Practice is not just part of the process; it *is* the process. You are not expected to master the law as a student. Frankly, this is impossible because the law is dynamic. Lawyers must apply an ever-changing array of legislation, regulations, and judicial decisions to new facts. Understanding how the pieces fit together requires practice in law school and beyond. This applies to nearly every area of law.

For example, employment lawyers must monitor changes in federal, state, and local laws to properly advise clients on how to maintain compliant workplaces. In the wake of the #MeToo and #TimesUp Movements, employers in virtually every industry were compelled to scrutinize their policies to eliminate discrimination and harassment in the workplace. While company-specific policies are needed to remove bad actors from organizations and create inclusive cultures, legislators in many states jumped into action by expanding workplace protections for sexual harassment. New York City, for example, now requires all employers with fourteen or more employees or independent contractors to provide mandatory sexual harassment training. Before the #MeToo Movement, employers commonly required complainants to sign confidentiality and non-disclosure provisions in agreements to settle harassment cases. Now, these types of provisions are prohibited unless they are included at the complainant's election. The purpose is to prevent companies and individuals from attempting to silence survivors.

As a law student, recognize that the *practice* of law involves a predictable pattern: we experiment, perhaps fail, learn something new, build confidence, and engage again. Legal practice and law school are not about *perfection*; they are about continuous improvement. Viewing law school as an opportunity to grow hopefully lightens the crippling weight of perfectionism. Yes, we want to produce excellent results.

But there is a difference between perfection and excellence. In the next section, let's explore what perfectionism is and how it can lead to feelings of imposterism.

Ditch The Idea Of Perfectionism

The American Psychological Association defines perfectionism as follows:

> *n.* the tendency to demand of others or of oneself an extremely high or even flawless level of performance, in excess of what is required by the situation. It is associated with depression, anxiety, eating disorders, and other mental health problems. —**perfectionist** *adj., n.*

Imposterism and perfectionism can feed off one another to create a negative feedback loop. Here's how it could play out: You lack confidence in your abilities, so you anxiously push yourself to produce work that is beyond reproach (i.e., perfect). When the work is not flawless, or if you make a mistake, this could reinforce the feeling of self-doubt.

Perfection does not exist; it's an illusion. Striving for it is futile. In fact, perfection can impede excellence. As a soon-to-be-lawyer, how do you distinguish perfectionism and excellence? Here's how I separate the two.

- Perfection is hypervigilance; excellence is due diligence.
- Perfection is setting myself up for failure; excellence is clearing a path for experimentation.
- In my body, perfection feels like pressure, contracting, clinching, tightening; excellence feels like openness and expansiveness.
- Perfection is unattainable; excellence is reachable.
- Perfection focuses on production; excellence celebrates achievements along the way.
- Perfection is all or nothing; excellence is making inch-by-inch advancements.

- Perfection is fear; excellence is creativity.

If you find yourself feeling like an imposter, ask whether you are reaching for the unattainable—perfection. This type of unhealthy striving can also lead to procrastination, rigidity, and comparison (more on that subject in chapter 6). None of these things will serve you in law school and may unintentionally fuel feelings of imposterism. Edith Eger, psychologist, and author of *The Gift* says it best: "If you're perfectionistic, you're competing with God. And you're human. You're going to make mistakes. Don't try to beat God, because God will always win."[5]

Some of the adages we internalized growing up may reinforce perfectionist tendencies. These cautionary tales from my upbringing come to mind:

Don't let them see you cry.
Don't let them see you sweat.
You've got to work twice as hard to get half as far.

These well-intentioned messages are trauma responses that unknowingly burden the recipient. Let me explain how these messages manifested for me.

- "Don't let them see you cry." Or "Don't let them see you sweat." *Translation:* Do not be emotional. If you ask for help or show any signs of vulnerability, you will not be taken seriously. What you show your employers, your professors, the world must be flawless.
- "You've got to work twice as hard to get half as far." *Translation:* Rest is a luxury beyond reach.

As a practicing lawyer, for the longest time, I struggled with taking regular vacations because of the well-meaning "advice" that I needed to outhustle my peers. Intellectually, I knew the importance of taking time off. In fact, when I mentored junior and mid-level associates at my firm, I would

[5] Edith Eger, *The Gift: 12 Lessons to Save Your Life* (New York: Scribner, 2020) 144.

plead with them to take regular vacations to reduce stress and prevent burnout. I would even help my mentees draft emails to their supervising partners to request time off.

Why was I ignoring my own advice? I viewed vacation as inconsistent with the precept to work "twice as hard." There was no way I could work twice as hard while relaxing on the beach in Greece. For years, I accepted the exhausting notion that vacations were not meant for me.

Recognize High-Effort Coping When It Appears

What I have just described has a name. It is called high-effort coping, "a behavioral style that those who are locked out of opportunities, due to racial and ethnic discrimination, tend to utilize to gain access and to prove their worth."[6] Epidemiologist Sherman James describes high-effort coping as a behavior going back to the Civil War that many Black people engaged in after Emancipation to prove their worth. James uses the term "John Henryism" to describe high-effort coping because it reminded him of the legend of John Henry, an American folk hero.

> According to the legend, John Henry was born into slavery, and after Emancipation became a laborer driving steel for the C&O Railroad. Steel drivers were those workers who hammered steel into rocks to make holes for explosives that blasted the rock so that a railroad tunnel could be constructed. As the story goes, John Henry was a giant of a man with superhuman strength, considered to be the strongest, fastest, and hardest worker on the rails. The legend tells us that in a man-against-machine contest to drill a hole through a mountain, to make way for a tunnel, John Henry, with only a nine-pound hammer in his hands, beat the mechanical drill. But when he hammered his way through the mountain and got to the

---

[6] Gail Parker, Ph. D., *Restorative Yoga for Ethnic and Race-Based Stress and Trauma*, (Singing Dragon, 2020) 67.

other side, he collapsed from exhaustion. His heart gave out and he died with his hammer in his hands.[7]

After about five years of working at a big law firm, not taking regular vacations was inexcusable. Rest may not always feel productive, but sometimes, taking a reprieve, yes, even in law school, is necessary.

Be Kind To Your Fellow Law Students

Cultivating compassion for others can buffer imposter sensations. My message here is simple: Be gracious to your fellow law students. Be a caregiver. Spread kindness. This advice may seem counterintuitive when it feels like you and your classmates have been unwillingly catapulted into the *Hunger Games*. But trust me, you will not regret offering an encouraging word to your peers. And your own subjective happiness may increase the more you practice kindness. Lasting friendships will naturally flow if you pay attention to those around you and find opportunities to humanize the experience. If someone confides in you, it's okay to say, "I understand what you mean," "I'm with you," "I get it," "I feel that way too," "Is there anything I can do?," "I'm lost too," or "Is there a way we can navigate this together?" The most comforting thing for a law student to hear (and to say), could be "I haven't started either." Vulnerability creates connection, and in law school, collect moments to stand arm-in-arm with those around you.

As psychologist Harriet Lerner reminds us, "Anxiety is extremely contagious, but so is calm." Look for opportunities to radiate peace. This steady presence will be in high demand and a welcome contrast to those teetering on the edge of a nervous breakdown. You can normalize and smooth out the rough edges of your new academic environment by noticing those around you. Be hyper-tuned in. It may seem strange to

[7] Nelson, S.R. *Steel Drivin' Man: John Henry, the Untold Story of an American Legend*, New York, NY: Oxford University Press (2006).

promote this unconventional idea of deliberate kindness to your fellow classmates when everything around you screams put your head down and grind. Yes, there will be a significant amount of work to do, but don't forget that your classmates are in this rewarding struggle with you. In fact, you have a unique opportunity to create the kind of profession that you want to work in.

Kindness is not complicated. I remember impatiently waiting in line at Starbucks one fall morning before my contracts class to get my liquid fuel for the day. The barista handed me a hot, grande caramel macchiato, which I held in one hand, and with the other, cradled my awkward 300-page contracts textbook on my hip. It was almost as if the barista shouted, "Hey you, 1L, your drink is ready." Noticing the trappings of a first-year student, a 3L I had never met, introduced herself, and we started talking. This student did not become my law school best friend, she wasn't a mentor in any official capacity, and she did not help me land my first job. It may not seem like a lot, but during my first year of law school, she consistently did four simple, yet powerful things.

She remembered my name.

She said hello to me every time we passed one another in the hallways.

She asked how I was doing.

She waited for me to answer. I mean, *really* answer. After the automatic response of "I'm doing fine," she would pause and allow space for the real answer to pour out.

I felt comfortable asking for her advice and she would always respond. This 3L is now a partner at a leading law firm in New York, and to this day, I can email her, and she'd ask how I am doing and wait for me to answer. I share this story to encourage you to search for seemingly small encounters that are meaningful ways to be present. This is also an important reminder when you become a 2L or 3L—be kind to people waiting in line for coffee.

Ask For Help, Engage A Tutor, And Embrace Legal Supplements

You can combat the imposter phenomenon by asking for help, registering for a tutor, and reviewing legal supplements to reinforce what you are learning. Students may feel like they do not belong or doubt their abilities because they have never organized information in a way that law school demands. That's expected! The way to address this is to dig into the material and ask for backup when you need it.

Ask For Help

One of the worst things you can do when feeling like an imposter is to isolate yourself. Lawyers are skilled in projecting confidence. They pride themselves on being able to speak definitively, write persuasively, and answer questions decisively (even when they are bluffing, trust me this happens). These qualities have their place, but we should also celebrate lawyers who ask for help. The reluctance to seek guidance often starts in law school and intensifies thereafter. Lawyers want to exude independence, and pride can get in the way of asking for help. But our accomplishments are not tainted or less impressive if we rely on others along the way. If we are too proud to ask for help, we may miss an easy way to lighten the load and create opportunities for connection. Think of it this way: if *clients* are too proud to seek guidance, the legal profession would be extinct. What if asking for guidance leads to something spectacular? What if a straightforward ask like, "Can I pick your brain on this?" bridges the gap between where you are and where you aspire to be? How might your life (and law school experience) improve if you were more open to asking for and receiving help, without ego-driven constraints?

Asking for help is also strategic. Adam Grant's book, *Give and Take, a Revolutionary Approach to Success*, insightfully explores the differences between takers, givers, and matchers.

According to Grant, asking for advice is an excellent way to build meaningful relationships because it allows others to contribute to your life and feel good about doing so. People love to be acknowledged for their expertise. When you ask for guidance, you get your questions answered and you simultaneously create an opportunity for others to shine as they share what they know. It's hard to go wrong here.

You can access support from multiple avenues in law school. Resources include the dean of students, student affairs, career advisors, alumni, professors, and, yes, even other students. If your health insurance covers therapy, coaching, or counseling services, consider talking to a professional, especially during challenging periods. The law school load, by itself, can be overwhelming. Add to that life events, many of which are beyond our control. People get married, pass away, get diagnosed with debilitating illnesses, have children, and celebrate birthdays, anniversaries, graduations, and other milestones. It is not always easy to show up in these moments, espeically when you are in law school, but know that help is a simple ask away.

Participate in Tutoring

One way to get support in law school is to sign up for tutoring programs. Tutors may have insight on the teaching styles of specific professors and can conduct sessions one-on-one or in small groups. Tutoring can also increase your engagement with the course material in an informal setting and provide confidence that you're on the right track. Tutoring programs may not appear in the orientation materials you receive, so don't be afraid to ask questions about resources that may not be advertised. If you don't want to participate in formal tutoring, consider joining or starting a study group to connect with others. This can make the daily law school grind more collaborative, even fun (well, "fun" by law school standards). An important caveat here: avoid study groups that are unfocused, disorganized, and make you feel incompetent or that you are not doing enough. Who needs that kind of energy? Instead, surround yourself with a nurturing group who will hold you accountable, challenge you, and force you to think gigantic, creative thoughts about meaningfully using the law. If this group does not exist, how can you create it?

If you join a study group, ensure that you are pulling your own weight. That means showing up on time, reading the cases in advance, and not expecting your classmates to pour into you without offering anything in return.

During my 1L year, I participated in tutoring sessions for civil procedure with other students from my section. I looked forward to this time where I could process information interactively and get help from—and give help to—my classmates. Our tutor explained convoluted concepts and refined conclusions we were making along the way. Law school demands an enormous amount of individual work, but this does not mean you have to (or should) march forward alone. Togetherness sweetens the adventure. Isolation can be dangerous.

Embrace Legal Supplements

Legal supplements distill jargon-filled cases into clear issues and conclusions of law. They provide the "aha moment" that demystifies what you are reading. When a client wants to know the answer to a question like, "Can I sue for breach of contract?" you must succinctly explain the elements of the law and how the facts of your case apply. I once had a client ask me to summarize a case and "forget my lawyer *condition*" when doing so, as if my legal training was an impairment to overcome. They wanted a quick and dirty analysis of why the case mattered and how it impacted them.

Back to supplements. The benefit is that they get to the heart of the matter, the essence of the case without the fluff. Depending on the class, you may find supplements that are linked to your case book. Supplements can be used before or after class lectures. For example, *before* reading your casebook, supplements can preview what you will read and give you a baseline understanding of the issues that will be discussed. You can also use supplemental materials *after* you have read the full case to confirm you understand a legal decision or principle. If, for some reason, you cannot read the entire case before class (and you should do everything in your power to stay on top of the reading), having a general understanding of the parties, the facts, and the legal issues will be helpful. Supplements are better than nothing.

So, why do supplements get a bad reputation? For one thing, supplements are not substitutes for reading your case book or attending class. You should not rely on these resources exclusively. Moreover, unless your professor wrote the supplement you are using, it may not shed light on your professors' approach to the cases and what they deem important for exam purposes. The only way to understand this is by attending class and daily wrestling with the material. There are no short cuts, remember?

In addition, no matter how detailed supplements are, they will not teach you how to think like a lawyer. After law school, you will not have supplements to rely on to dissect cases for you. My best advice is to use supplements as a resource, not a crutch.

Act Like You Belong

Even if you feel like an imposter, don't act like one. Walk tall, push your shoulders back and away from your ears, and lift your head up high. Breathe deeply from your diaphragm.

On a physical level, it is easy to identify people who command attention when they walk into a room. We also know what this looks like in the opposite direction: sitting with arms folded across the chest, crossing the legs, and slouching the shoulders forward. Any posture that makes us look itty bitty. How often do we pay attention to the space we occupy? Certainly gender norms and societal expectations impact the degree to which we decide to spread out. Whether it's based on a desire to play it small or blend in, though, you can practice expansion.

Consider all the ways you can practice shining in law school. How can you be expansive with your thoughts, ideas, dreams, speech, and writing? Is your generosity spacious? When do you tend to advance versus retreat, release instead of clench, exude rather than collapse? What is this decision based on?

Get comfortable acting like you belong. After a few years of practice, I had an eureka moment when drafting an email to a partner regarding our litigation strategy. I started the email by stating, "My two cents are…" Shameful! Here I was, a senior associate at a large law firm, billing hundreds of dollars an hour, cheapening my input to two measly cents. Why was I devaluing my contribution and signaling to the partner that my suggestion wasn't worth listening to? I deleted that useless lead-in and vowed to let my words stand on their own. How many of these phrases can you eliminate from your communications?

- "For what it's worth…"
- "This may not be [relevant, important, a winner], but I think we should ____."
- "This idea probably isn't [the best one, the most practical, feasible], but____."
- "This is just my opinion."
- "I may be off base here, but what if we tried it this way."
- "I could be wrong here, but _____."
- Saying "I think" when you know for sure. For example, "I think the deadline to answer the complaint is October 17," when you have double and triple checked the docket, and confirmed that this is, in fact, the deadline.

- At the end of sentences, asking "does that make sense?""
Let me answer that for you. Yes, you make sense. Let
your words stand.

These disclaimers rest on the faulty premise that your
contributions are not valuable. If you are sharing your views,
you have something meaningful to offer. So, why waste
words and detract from your message?

Humility is a virtue, yes. And deference, in some situations, may be warranted. But constantly using crippling
language can hijack opportunities and leave you overlooked,
overshadowed, or underpaid. Taking up space isn't always
neat and tidy. It's messy, relentless, commanding, irreverent,
undiluted, and at times unruly. Sometimes that's what true
expansion calls for. That is stretched living. That is what I
want for you in law school and beyond. In *Braving the Wilderness*, Brené Brown writes:

> Stop walking through the world looking for confirma-
> tion that you don't belong. You will always find it because
> you've made that your mission. Stop scouring people's
> faces for evidence that you're not enough. You will al-
> ways find it because you've made that your goal. True
> belonging and self-worth are not goods; we don't nego-
> tiate their value with the world. The truth about who we
> are lives in our hearts. Our call to courage is to protect
> our wild heart against constant evaluation, especially our
> own. No one belongs here more than you.[8]

An imposter attitude will make you think and act like a miniature version of the student (and lawyer) you are meant to
be. Expand to fill the room; resist shrinking to make yourself
(or others) comfortable. There will be many opportunities
for you to exercise your divinely inspired boldness. Tiptoe,
step, or leap—just get there. And when you arrive, know be-

[8] Brené Brown, *Braving the Wilderness: The Quest for True Belonging and the Courage to Stand Alone* (New York: Random House, 2017) 158.

yond the shadow of a doubt that you have earned the right to S-P-R-E-A-D O-U-T and shine!

Solo Sidebar

In the courtroom, a "sidebar" is an area in front of the judge's bench outside of earshot from the jury and witnesses. A sidebar gives the judge and attorneys a chance to address issues privately, sometimes off the record (meaning without the stenographer transcribing the dialogue). At the end of each chapter, I invite you to answer questions to help you discover ways you can show up for yourself. Every now and then, we need to have honest conversations with ourselves to forge ahead. These "Solo Sidebars," followed by a concluding mindfulness practice, will help you do just that.

1. Make your own list of the differences between perfection and excellence. How does your body feel when you pursue perfection versus excellence?

2. When you need to remember how qualified you are, what activities, accomplishments, and triumphs will you use to populate your "anti-imposter" list? Some accomplishments are public—the promotions, graduations, and awards. Others, only you know about. For example, maybe you did the right thing when no one was looking. Maybe you implemented a system or habit that you consistently applied. Celebrate these successes.

3. Where do you tend to play it small? In your speech? In written communications? In your body? In your thinking? In your ambition? What steps can you take to be more dynamic? What does "owning it" look like?

4. Make a list of uplifting mantras, scriptures, quotes and/or prayers that you will re-read or recite to yourself to stop the noise of the imposter phenomenon in its tracks.

5. When feelings of imposterism arise, with whom can you confide? If no one comes to mind, what resources does your law school offer to support you?

Concluding Mindfulness Practice: 4-4-8 Ratio Breathing

If you are new to meditation, yoga, or other contemplative practices, recognizing the power of your breath is transformative. Some bodily functions operate automatically, such as our heartbeat, digestion, sweating, and shivering. We do not have to think about our heart sending electrical signals that cause different parts of the muscle to expand and contract; it pumps blood to our entire body, on its own, without concentrated effort. Other actions require deliberate decision making like lifting your arms over your head. Breathing enjoys a category of its own—it is an automatic bodily function *and* something we can consciously control.

The benefits of deep, focused breathing include better stress management, increased focus, lower blood pressure, and an overall sense of ease and well-being. As a law student, you can creatively incorporate deep belly breaths into your daily routine. For example, every time your professor uses a Latin word in class, or you read one in your textbook, let this spark a reminder to take two, full, deep, uninterrupted breaths.

Consider "stacking" breathing cues on top of an existing habit. Researchers call this an "anchoring activity." Here's how it works: identify a well-ingrained positive habit you have already established. Maybe that habit is making your bed every morning, brushing your teeth, or making coffee. Now, pick another habit that you want to incorporate and "stack" that activity on top of the existing routine. After making your bed each morning, you can add, for example, a short breathing exercise or movement to start your day.

At the end of each chapter, I will offer a mix of breathing, stretching, relaxation, and mindfulness exercises to experiment with before or after class, in the library, while waiting in line for coffee or commuting, or in the privacy of your own home. Several exercises incorporate conscious breathing reminders. Let me preempt a question you may have: why focus on the breath? Our breath is always with us; it grounds us; and can encourage us to be more present-minded.

Our first practice is a 4:4:8 breathing exercise, where we inhale for four seconds, pause for four counts and exhale for eight seconds. By intentionally lengthening our exhales, we activate the parasympathetic nervous system (which is responsible for the rest and digest function).

To begin, find a comfortable position, sitting in a chair or standing up. Lengthen your spine by imagining a string that is connected to the crown of your head. As you inhale, visualize someone gently pulling the string so that your torso lengthens two additional inches toward the sky. Relax your entire body, including the muscles in your face. When you are ready, add the breath.

- Inhale through your nose for a count of four, allowing your belly and ribcage to slowly expand.
- As effortlessly as you can, pause your breath for a count of four.
- On a count of eight, completely expel the air through your nose or mouth. If the environment is appropriate, as you exhale, add an audible sigh, flutter the lips, or even hum to accentuate your exhale. Vocalizations can help release tension in the throat, which can become restricted when stressed.
- Repeat this sequence three to four times in a row.

You can do this exercise with your eyes open or closed. Remember to keep your shoulders, jaw, and any other part of your body that is holding tension, relaxed. Customization is key. For example, if you feel anxious while pausing your breath for four counts or if eight beats is too long to exhale, please tweak this exercise (and any others) to meet your individual needs.

2

ANCHOR YOUR LAW SCHOOL EXPERIENCE IN GRATITUDE

Gratitude is a potent antidote to negativity, because it doesn't depend on your life circumstances. You could be poor and starving and yet still grateful for a warm breeze.

—Alex Korb

Law school is nothing like undergrad. In college, you had multiple opportunities to demonstrate mastery over course concepts—homework assignments, research papers, quizzes, class participation, midterms, finals, and if you were lucky, extra credit. In law school, however, typically one exam (or final paper) determines your entire grade. Let me not mince words—this work is demanding.

To respond to the unique challenges law school presents, invest in the best coping mechanism there is—gratitude. This chapter describes what gratitude is, encourages you to make it a staple of your law school toolkit, and offers strategies to cultivate more of it.

Sonja Lyubomirsky, professor of psychology, exquisitely describes gratitude this way:

> It is wonder; it is appreciation; it is looking at the bright side of a setback; it is fathoming abundance; it is thanking someone in your life; it is thanking God; it is counting blessings. It is savoring; it is not taking things for granted; it is coping; it is present-oriented. Gratitude is an antidote to negative emotions, a neutralizer of envy, hostility, worry, and irritation.[9]

[9] Sonja Lyubomirsky, *The How of Happiness: A New Approach to Getting*

When our personal and professional to-do lists are spiraling out of control, gratitude probably is not a priority. But you can experience moments of calm by anchoring your law school journey in the transformative benefits of gratitude. Even on our worst days, there will always be something or someone to appreciate. For starters, you can appreciate the people in your support system, those who regularly pour life-affirming energy into you. Whatever you call them— your cheerleader, squad, crew, network, tribe, personal board of directors, or "amen corner"—write their names down.

Ask #2: Identify your law school support system.

This list, your personal Super PAC (Personal Affirmation Committee), will be an important lifeline during law school, and I encourage you to let these individuals know, in advance, that you may need their support. When you have this person or group of people in mind, you are rooted in gratitude, making it impossible to be grateful and anxious at the same time. Try it—you cannot entertain thoughts of appreciation and unease simultaneously.

Celebrate Your Student Status

Trust me, I did not appreciate *everything* about being a law school student. Unlike college, weekends in law school were merely an extension of the school week. There were many days when I was overwhelmed, eyes blurry and fatigued from studying. Even on the weekends, it was difficult to completely disconnect. One Friday night, I remember leaving the library around midnight with my friend Michelle. As we sleepily meandered to our respective apartments, Michelle and I enviously passed slews of carefree undergraduate students, making their way to the nearest decompression zone, eager to blow off steam from the week they just survived. These undergrads were immaculately dressed and accessorized— everything from head to toe was perfectly coordinated. Mi-

the Life You Want (New York: Penguin Press, 2007).

chelle and I accessorized too. We proudly donned stuffed book bags on our backs and toted oversized case books in our hands.

I complained to Michelle, "It's torture watching everyone else live their best lives while we spend our Friday night as hostages in the library. Being immersed in this abstract stuff is exhausting." My whining almost unleashed a domino effect of complaints. But instead of participating in my wallowing, Michelle started celebrating our student status. Michelle responded, "There is something special about where we are right now. We get to attend this three-year program and take our time learning as much as we can. We don't 'have to' be here. We 'get to' simply be students. We worked for this opportunity and are making a choice to invest in our legal education."

Continuing her late-night epiphany, Michelle added, "After graduation, we will be responsible for solving high-stakes problems. If we make a mistake representing a real client, there will be consequences. Getting it wrong may cost someone their freedom, livelihood, reputation, or millions of dollars in damages. Even if our representation is masterful, we do not control judges or juries. Thankfully, we do not have to worry about any of that now, and I don't want to rush it." Though I did not appreciate Michelle's insight in the moment (it was actually annoying at the time), she didn't want me to overlook how fortunate we were to be in law school as it was unfolding.

There is a difference between *feeling* grateful and *being* grateful. Law school won't always *feel* gratifying, but I challenge you to embrace gratitude. This requires deliberate effort. You may not *feel* grateful when you have one hundred pages of constitutional law to read, a paper to submit, and personal responsibilities demanding your attention. But you can be grateful for the in-between steps—when you completed the assigned reading, finished a rough draft of a final paper, or read ahead for a class. In everything, we can allow gratitude to permeate space that would otherwise be overgrown by worry. We can control our gratitude practice. According to theologian and psychologist Henri Nouwen, gratitude is a choice.

> I can choose to be grateful even when my emotions and feelings are steep and hurt and resentful. It is amazing how many occasions present themselves in which I can choose gratitude instead of a complaint. I can choose to be grateful when I am criticized, even when my heart responds in bitterness. . . . I can choose to listen to the voices that forgive and to look at the faces that smile, even while I still hear words of revenge and see grimaces of hatred.[10]

Practicing gratitude rewires the brain—that's transformational! Alex Korb, neuroscientist, coach, and author of the book *The Upward Spiral: Using Neuroscience to Reverse the Course of Depression One Small Change at a Time*, describes a "gratitude circuit" in our brain that we can strengthen.[11] As you develop this muscle in law school, it will be readily available as a practicing attorney. Gratitude releases dopamine, the pleasure hormone responsible for making us feel "great both physically and emotionally."[12] After receiving a hit of dopamine, the brain's reward system helps us remember the behavior that caused the dopamine to be released. This process engages our brain in what Korb calls "a virtuous cycle." The more you express gratitude, the more dopamine is released, and

---

[10] Henri J. M. Nouwen, *The Return of the Prodigal Son: A Story of Homecoming* (Doubleday, 1994) 69.

[11] Alex Korb, *The Upward Spiral: Using Neuroscience to Reverse the Course of Depression, One Small Change at a Time* (Oakland, CA: New Harbinger Publications, Inc., 2015) 152.

[12] Paula Felps, *Gratitude Can Improve our Physical, Mental and Emotional Health*, LIVE HAPPY MAGAZINE, http://www.livehappy.com/sites/default/files/LH1412_GRATITUDE_sm.pdf.

the more your brain will desire the pleasurable activity.[13] The more we focus on negative events, the more ingrained the neural pathways for undesirable thinking become. Gratitude guides us in the opposite direction, helping us identify and build on what is going right.[14] Gratitude allows anxiety to dissipate because it is difficult to concentrate on two conflicting states simultaneously.[15] We simply lack the bandwidth to divide our limited attention between extremes.

Gratitude Is Not About Playing Dodge Ball With Your Emotions

We have spent the last few pages talking about what gratitude is. A quick word on what it is *not*.

- Good vibes only.
- It could be worse.
- Stay positive.
- Don't be a negative Nancy or Ned.
- Be optimistic.
- There's always a silver lining.
- Look on the bright side.
- Insert your favorite toxically positive phrase here.

Toxic Positivity Is Real

As you elevate gratitude, I am not suggesting that you invalidate unpleasant emotions you may experience in law school or in any other arena. If you're exhausted after pulling an all-nighter, you're tired. If you are disappointed, upset, or frustrated after getting a certain grade, that is a real emotion. Experience that. And no matter what employer or client down the line tries to convince you otherwise, you have permission to fully process what comes up.

Gratitude is not about silencing your emotions and encour-

---

[13] Korb, *The Upward Spiral*, at 151.

[14] Emily Fletcher, *The Neuroscience of Gratitude*, Huffington Post, http://www.huffingtonpost.com/emily-fletcher/the-neuroscience-of-gratitude_b_8631392.html.

[15] Korb, *The Upward Spiral*, at 151.

aging you to see the bright side no matter the circumstances. Gratitude is not about faking it. In fact, burying what you feel can also morph into maladaptive coping mechanisms.

Sometimes our emotions, even the ones we do not want to confront, are informative. Does the feeling mean we should make an adjustment? Is this emotion providing insight into what aligns with our values, goals, and passions? What actions do we need to take, if any, to honor the emotions that bubble up?

Let's not confuse gratitude with toxic positivity. Gratitude is connected to something real. Toxic positivity is denial. It is pretending that what you are feeling isn't worthy of attention. Gratitude surveys the entire spectrum of emotions, and rather than ignore the negative, gratitude allows you to see it all—the marvelous, the hot mess, and everything in between. With an appreciation lens, you can choose to focus on what is going right.

[Optimism] is not about providing a recipe for self-deception. The world can be a horrible, cruel place, and at the same time it can be wonderful and abundant. These are both truths. There is not a halfway point; there is only choosing which truth to put in your personal foreground.

—Lee Ross

Cultivate Gratitude In Law School

How can you cultivate gratitude in law school? In this section, I will provide three evidence-based approaches to strengthen your gratitude practice. The benefits of gratitude are no longer theoretical. Study after study has demonstrated that consistent expressions of appreciation increase our overall wellbeing and strengthen our relationships. Given what we know about the demonstrated benefits of expressing gratitude, why don't we lean into this practice? One explanation is that we tend to resist the small habits that can make us objectively healthier. We know that drinking water is good for us; yet many people are dehydrated. We know the value of good quality sleep; yet most people are sleep deprived. We also know that people who write down their goals are more likely to achieve them; yet people dream without writing anything down. Simple tasks, like a regular gratitude practice, can be your superpower.

Gratitude Journaling

Law school is a great time to start a written gratitude journal (or gratitude listing). I know, I know, it sounds too basic to make a difference, but this practice is backed by scientific research. In a 2003 study examining the benefits of inducing gratitude, participants were divided into three groups—one group was asked to write down what they were grateful for daily; another recorded their daily hassles; and the third group listed neutral life events. Researchers Robert Emmons and Michael McCullough found that the gratitude group reported a more positive outlook on life and engaged in more physical activity compared to the other two groups.[16] So what does this mean for you? Grab a notebook or find an application on your phone to regularly record your blessings.

Consider all there is to celebrate in law school.

- Unfettered access to professors who are experts in their respective fields.
- The opportunity to discuss historic and current events with prominent lawyers, professors, legal commentators, and scholars. Many law schools frequently invite practitioners to discuss hot legal topics. Make time to attend these events.
- The chance to think deeply about how you can use the law as a tool to create change.
- Lasting personal and professional relationships.

[16] Emmons, R.A., & McCullough, M.E. (2003). Counting Blessings versus burdens: An experimental investigation of gratitude and subjective well-being in daily life. *Journal of Personality and Social Psychology*, 84, 377-389.

- If applicable, the ability to live in and explore a new city.
- Access to your law school's vast alumni network, many of whom would be willing to speak to law students and offer advice.
- The luxury of dressing like a student for three years.
- Time to explore areas of the law that excite you.
- Grants, scholarships, and, yes, even loans to help finance your legal education.

Gratitude Letter-Writing

Another strategy to strengthen your gratitude muscle is to write a heartfelt letter to someone you appreciate. A 2011 study involving over 200 participants "examined the effects of writing letters of gratitude on three primary qualities of well-being: happiness (positive affect), life-satisfaction (cognitive evaluation), and depression (negative affect)."[17] The outcome? Writing letters of gratitude increased participants' happiness and life satisfaction, while decreasing depressive symptoms. You may not have time to pen lengthy gratitude letters in law school, but you can receive similar uplifting benefits by sending people you appreciate emails, cards, or even text messages to show your thankfulness.[18]

Savoring Walks

In 2007, researchers Fred Bryant and Joseph Veroff conducted a study at Loyola University Chicago where they asked participants to take a "savoring walk" every day for a week. Savoring is deliberate effort to notice, appreciate, and prolong positive experiences. When researchers later as-

---

[17] Steven Toepfer, Kelly Cichy, and Patti Peters, 2012. "Letters of Gratitude: Further Evidence for Author Benefits," Journal of Happiness Studies, Springer, vol. 13(1), 187-201, March.

[18] Fred Bryant and Joseph Veroff, Savoring: A new model of positive experience. Mahwah, New Jersey: Lawrence Erlbaum Associates, Inc. (2007).

sessed the participants, they found an increase in the group's overall happiness.[19]

As you begin your law school journey, actively look for experiences to savor. Commit to sharpening your gratitude muscle. While you will soon learn case briefing techniques, exam taking strategies, and what it means to "think like a lawyer," let gratitude anchor you. Magnificent moments worth cherishing will be all around you, waiting to be noticed. In everything you do, practice gratitude.

Solo Sidebar

1. What excites you the most about starting law school?
2. Write down the names of the people in your Super PAC (Personal Affirmation Committee). What do you appreciate about them? Do they know you are about to start law school? What conversations can you have with your Super PAC now about how they can support you in law school?
3. Create a pre-law school gratitude list. What are you thankful for before law school has even started?
4. Consider the differences between gratitude and toxic positivity. How can you encourage yourself to express authentic gratitude without suppressing or attempting to escape negative emotions?

Concluding Mindfulness Practice: Compassionate Touch

For this practice, I want to build on the 4-4-8 ratio breathing exercise we explored in the previous chapter. To recap, breathe in for four counts; pause for four beats; and expel the air out for eight counts. As you flow through this 4-4-8 breathing pattern, I invite you to place your hands in positions on your body, if that feels calming. Dr. Kristin Neff,

---

[19] Fred Bryant and Joseph Veroff, *Savoring: A new model of positive experience*. Mahwah, New Jersey: Lawrence Erlbaum Associates, Inc. (2007).

an Associate Professor of Educational Psychology at the University of Texas at Austin, is a leading researcher and pioneer in the field of self-compassion. Dr. Neff highlights that, with compassionate self-touch, our brains do not distinguish between whether a loving touch is coming from a close friend or from ourselves. Because physical touch releases oxytocin, compassionate self-holds can provide a calming way to self-soothe while observing the ebb and flow of the breath. In addition, if you feel tension or fatigue in a specific area of the body, you can place your hand on that spot to encourage a release. My favorite self-holds are below.

- Cradle your face in your hands by placing one or both hands on your cheeks.

- Gently stroke your arms from your biceps to elbows. If it feels soothing, give your arms a gentle squeeze.

- Lightly rub the area over your heart using slow circular movements.

- Place one or both hands on your belly and feel it rise and fall under the weight of your hands.

- Place one hand over your heart and another on the belly. With each inhale, experience the rise of the chest and stomach and with each exhale, envision yourself further surrendering to the breath.

- Rest one hand on your forehead and the other on the back of your neck, palm facing down.

Explore other hand variations that feel nourishing and grounding. As you move through these exercises, notice the weight of your hands, the warmth they elicit and, perhaps, express gratitude for the support each part of your body offers as you engage in these compassionate self-holds.

3

IT TAKES A VILLAGE TO SUPPORT A LAWYER

Everyone needs a support system, be it family, friends, coworkers, therapists, or religious leaders. We cannot do life alone and expect to keep mentally, emotionally, and spiritually healthy. Everyone needs some sort of support system on which to rely.

—Richelle E. Goodrich

In the last chapter, we discussed the importance of assembling a reliable support system to pour into you over the next three years. That sounds wonderful in theory, but in practice, what if your confidants don't understand the increased pressure you will face in law school? What if no one in your community attended law school and the extent of their "knowledge" comes from hit shows like "Law and Order" or "How to Get Away with Murder"? What if they do not know how to hold space for you? Their well-intentioned advice that you "shouldn't work too hard," that you "need to sleep eight hours," or that you "should carve out more time for yourself" may actually intensify the pressure, or worse, make you feel guilty if their suggestions feel impossible. Your village may not know where to start. Truth be told, *you* may have difficulty articulating what you need, so how can others be expected to step up? A "wait and see" approach is perfectly fine. But with a smidge of worthwhile work on the front end, you can prepare your supporters for what is to come.

After reading this chapter, you will have specific questions and conversation starters to share with your village so they can show up and shine with and for *you*.

Ask #3: Start Conversations with Your Personal Affirmation Committee

Revisit the list of individuals you identified as part of your Super PAC. After you have this list in hand, schedule a call with members of your tribe and explicitly ask for their encouragement before you start law school.

Send Your Law School Acceptance Letter To Your Super PAC

Refer to chapter 1 and explain to your loved ones that your law school acceptance letter is a tangible reminder that you have earned your seat. During the semester, ask your cheerleaders to periodically send the letter back to you with an encouraging note.

Identify What Works, Then Amplify It

Build on what works. For example, in college, if you were disciplined in reading your notes after every class, continue doing so. Similarly, if a loved one showed up in special ways during college, shine an appreciative spotlight on what they did. Be explicit. Make them aware of their specific actions and how their encouragement benefited you. To get you thinking, consider questions like this. What did you truly need the most while in college? What did your loved one remind you of when you were confronted with new challenges? What forms of support (financial or otherwise) did you receive during college or any other period of stress or transition? If you found those forms of support helpful, ask your community to continue uplifting you in this way.

Encourage Your Support System to Ask Gratitude-provoking Questions

You know from chapter 2 that gratitude increases wellbeing. Your community can help spark gratitude in the questions they ask, such as, with whom are you making memories in law school? Tell me about the last photo you took that made you smile? What are you grateful for today? What are you grateful for this week that came as a surprise to you? Recently, what made you chuckle or laugh out loud hysterically? What is improving or getting easier as the weeks in law school go by? What are you looking forward to? Tell me about something you are enjoying about law school. Who inspires you the most right now? What is currently exciting you?

The power behind these questions is that you can ask your support system to share their own responses, which creates a reciprocal flow of gratitude for you and your Super PAC.

Send Your Loved Ones A Link to Your Law School's Website

Before you start law school, arm your support system with as much information as possible. Send them a link to your law school's website and highlight where they can find the academic calendar, law school departments, and a list of resources available to support students. Although you will receive this information during orientation, as the semester progresses, you may forget what resources are available. And then, voilà, your loved ones are ready to step in and remind you that you're not alone.

Ask Your Support System to Help You Set Micro Goals

Consider asking your support system to help you break down goals into bite sized action items, especially as you add extracurriculars to your plate. For example, you may decide to write on a legal journal, participate in moot court, clinics, internships, clerkships, or perform pro bono work. Juggling your academic responsibilities, extracurricular activities, job interviews, and personal commitments may be overwhelming. Your loved ones can talk through your short-term goals and help you solidify the next steps to achieve them. Your Super PAC can ask you questions such as: Do you have any specific goals this week/month/semester? What can I do to help you achieve that goal? What upcoming decisions do you have to make? How can I help you with those decisions? Would it be helpful if we brainstormed together?

Know Your Love Language

Dr. Gary Chapman, author of the New York Times best-selling book, *The 5 Love Languages*, describes five ways in which we give and receive love: (1) acts of service (performing actions like chores, errands, or other tasks that show you care); (2) gifts (giving or receiving thoughtful gifts, which do not need to be extravagant); (3) quality time (giving someone your undivided attention when they are with you); (4) words of affirmation (providing verbal expressions of affection in the form of compliments or words of encouragement); and (5) physical touch (showing someone you care through physical gestures like hugs, a hand on the shoulder, or other forms of physical affection). Although Dr. Chapman's book focuses on romantic relationships, in my perspective, his framework can apply to friendships and familial relationships. We can strengthen our bonds with others by communicating with them using their specific "love language."

Before you start law school, determine what your love language is and share this information with your Super PAC. With this knowledge, your loved ones can tailor their support for you in law school.

For example, if you feel especially cared for by receiving gifts, your support system can lean into this love language. If you are going through a particularly stressful period, even the smallest time saver can have a significant impact. Here are a few gifts in the "time saving" category: laundry and apartment cleaning services, providing gift certificates to restaurants located near your loved one's law school. Other gifts can include stationary, coffee, gift cards, blue-light glasses (to help alleviate the strain on the eyes from looking at computer screens), travel mugs, sustainable water bottles, an extra phone charger, journals, yoga mat, groceries, massage certificates, fitness classes, and professional attire for networking events and interviews.

"How Can I Pray For You?" or "How Can I Support You?"

When talking to your loved ones, you may not know how to ask for what you need. To unearth some of these needs, your support system can ask you questions such as, how can I make you feel loved this week? How can I support you? What would be most helpful to you? How can I pray for you? You can even invite your loved one to pray for you, out loud, immediately after you share the concern. This is a special way for your community to take what you have shared and immediately cover you with words of hope and encouragement. If you or your loved one are not religious, your Super PAC can send positive thoughts your way and then verbalize those expressions to you.

Your Community Is Your Self-Care Accountability Partner

Law school is the perfect time to establish self-care practices. In chapter 4, we will delve deeper into what self-care is and curate a personalized self-care roadmap. For now, a simple definition will suffice. Self-care is recognizing what your mind, body, and soul need, and then tending to those needs with compassion. Plain and simple. After you create your self-care plan, share it with your loved ones so they can hold you accountable. Your community can ask questions like this: How did you practice self-care this week? What daily rituals are you engaged in? What can I do to support your self-care plan? Would it be helpful if we brainstormed ideas together?

You need community. While your village is there to uplift you, you must invest time and energy to communicate what you may need. With this chapter, you now have tools to help fortify your community, so they effectively support you.

Solo Sidebar

If you need help identifying your Super PAC, please do not panic. You have options! Here are three questions to help you find your law school tribe.

1. Who do you need to reconnect with? A former mentor, teacher, or classmate? Who was instrumental in your growth and development who would love to hear from you? From this list, who could you ask to support you during law school?

2. Consider asking the individuals who wrote your letters of recommendation for college or law school to join your Super PAC. Letters of recommendation are typically part of students' application materials, meaning *everyone* should have a list of potential law school supporters.

3. Don't forget about peer support in law school and on-campus resources. Go online and browse the list of law school staff in various departments. Identify two or three people and ask them if they would be willing to be part of your personal law school team.

Concluding Mindfulness Practice: Shoulder Lifts

In this mindfulness practice, we will focus on an area of the body that often holds tension: the shoulders. Many people unconsciously hike up their shoulders when stressed. Add to that, poor posture from long periods of sitting, hunched over our devices. The following exercise can help minimize stiffness in the shoulders, while connecting our breath to movement.

Begin by sitting or standing comfortably. Draw your navel toward your spine as you engage your core. Slightly lift your chest from your sternum. Breathe in through your nose for a count of four while simultaneously lifting your shoulders up to meet your ear lobes. As you exhale the air out on a slow and steady count of eight, release your shoulders down, creating as much space between your shoulders and ears. Notice the difference. Repeat this two-part sequence until your shoulders feel at ease and less tense.

4

Control the Controllables, and Be at Peace with the Rest

Everything is figureoutable.

—Marie Forleo

By now, you know that law school will be rigorous. As demanding as this quest will be, it is also completely "figureoutable." Knowing what to expect will prepare you for the bumps you may encounter along the way.

Imagine that one of your witnesses is scheduled to be deposed in two weeks. The deponent—the person who provides testimony under oath—has never testified before. He is visibly nervous, his voice shakes every time he answers a question, and he frankly wants nothing to do with the case. You must prepare the witness for what is to come—what questions will be asked, how they could be presented based on the lawyer's style (i.e., aggressively, conversationally), and what documents the deponent may have to explain. You also must ask the hard questions—the ones that may make the witness squirm. The purpose in asking the tough questions is not to scare the witness, but rather to increase their confidence in how to approach thorny aspects of the deposition.

For someone who has never been deposed, you may even describe what the conference room will look like and where the participants will be seated so the jittery witness will have familiarity with the room before they walk in. The best "depo prep sessions" empower the witness to focus on what they can control and normalize emotions that may arise. With sufficient preparation, before your client is sworn in to testify, they will know what is to come and find comfort knowing that everything will be okay.

The purpose of pre-framing, whether for a deposition or beginning law school, is to invite ease into unfamiliar and potentially uncomfortable experiences. Before law school starts, the more information you have, the less time you will spend asking questions like, "Is this normal?" or "Am I the only one who feels [overwhelmed, overworked, anxious, out of place, frustrated, exhausted, etc.]?" I don't want law school to surprise you, and I certainly don't want you grasping for a life jacket when you are already in the middle of the deep blue sea.

After reading this chapter, you will have a better understanding of what makes law school the worthwhile challenge it is and gain insight into what you *can* control as a law student. So, let's get to it.

Is Law School Really That Hard?

What makes law school the sweat-inducing experience that it is? Every student has experiences and specific temperaments they bring into the classroom. Regardless of one's background, the very structure of the law school academic environment—the Socratic method, minimal feedback, emphasis on competition, and the sheer amount of work—can be disorienting.

Researchers have studied why law school is often described as a challenging period. According to Cathaleen Roach, Assistant Dean for Educational Services at DePaul University College of Law, "up to 40 percent of law students may experience depression or other symptoms as a result of the law school experience."[20] Psychologists and educational theorists have hypothesized that some law students may be

---

[20] Cathaleen A. Roach, *A River Runs Through It: Tapping Into the Informational Stream to Move Students From Isolation to Autonomy*, 36 Ariz. L. Rev. (1994) 667.

predisposed to anxiety-prone behaviors, stemming from their natural inclination to achieve in everything they do.[21] (Another shout-out to my Type A readers.) Others believe that certain teaching methods unique to the law school experience place "enormous amounts of emotional stress on students that negatively affect, perhaps irreparably, students' self-esteem, their ability to perform, their short-term and long-term health, and their ultimate satisfaction with the [legal] profession."[22]

Law school is also challenging because it may be the first time students must think about every possible worst-case scenario, no matter how plausible. In fact, if there were awards given to those who can imagine every potential calamitous outcome, lawyers would win the "Worst-Case Visionary Award" every year. Lawyers brilliantly envision the worst. In representing clients, lawyers attempt to plan for every possibility—some would say this is what it means to "think like a lawyer." This exercise involves spotting legal issues and asking, what if this goes wrong? What am I missing? Is this witness's account credible? Who is at fault? Who can we hold liable? What if the person or entity we hold liable goes bankrupt? Will we still be able to collect on a monetary judgment? Can this legal advice backfire, and if so, how can I recalibrate without my client losing confidence in my abilities or without losing this case? What is the contingency plan if the first strategy I pursue fails?

Lawyers want to ensure that all bases are covered to avoid disappointing their client, getting fired, sued for malpractice, or tarnishing their reputation. Lawyering in a consistent state of hypervigilance and heightened scrutiny can wreak havoc on the nervous system. Constant attentiveness to what can

---

[21] Matthew M. Dammeyer & Narina Nunez, *Anxiety and Depression Among Law Students: Current Knowledge and Future Directions*, 23 L. & Human Behavior (1999) 55.

[22] Ruth Ann McKinney, *Depression and Anxiety in Law Students: Are We Part of the Problem and Can we be Part of the Solution?* (2003) 2.

go wrong, how it can go wrong, and the consequences of the wrong action can be all consuming.

It is easy to see how constantly thinking this way can lead to personal and professional unhappiness. In a 2000 study titled, "Countering Lawyer Unhappiness: Pessimism, Decision Latitude and the Zero-Sum Dilemma," researchers Paul R. Verkuil, Martin Seligman, and Terry Kang share the following:

> Unfortunately, what makes for a good lawyer may make for an unhappy human being. People cannot easily turn off their pessimism when they leave the office. Lawyers who can see acutely how bad things might be for clients are also burdened with the tendency to see how bad things might be for themselves. Pessimists are more likely than optimists to believe they will not make partner, that their profession is a racket, that their spouse is unfaithful or that the economy is headed for disaster. In this manner, pessimism that might be adaptive in the profession also carries the risk of a high toll of depression and anxiety in one's personal life. The challenge is to remain prudent professionally and yet contain these pessimistic tendencies in domains of life outside the office.[23]

Here's the challenge I offer to you. As you grapple with what it means to think like a lawyer, ask yourself whether that requires thinking like a perpetual pessimist. Yes, being exhaustive and strategic are important, but what else can we add to our analytical toolbox? These questions can help:

- If we pursued this strategy instead of another what could go right?
- What's the best possible outcome here? How can we

---

[23] Paul Verkuil, Martin Seligman, and Terry Kang, "Countering Lawyer Unhappiness: Pessimism, Decision Latitude and the Zero-Sum Dilemma" (September 2000). Available at SSRN: https://ssrn.com/abstract=241942.

work backward from there?

- What does success look like for this client, litigation, deal, transaction, or policy?

Strategic lawyering involves asking these questions to determine what can go right. In other words, see the potential problems as well as the possibilities.

With all the challenges law school presents (and many exist), remember to *control the controllables* and be at peace with the rest. So, what *can* you control as a 1L? The balance of this chapter answers this question.

Eat Well, Move Your Body, And Get Quality Rest

Let's start with the basics: eat decently, exercise regularly, and rest well. You already know these things, so I will not spend pages describing the value of these simple, yet not always easy, practices within your power. Some students (and practicing lawyers) get so engrossed in their work that they forget to eat or drink water. How can you expect to think critically, comprehend complicated case law, and move with efficiency throughout your day? You cannot. Not for any sustainable period, anyway.

Be intentional about how you treat your body. Lawyers invest significant amounts of time thinking about the impact of their legal advice, how their written and oral communications will be perceived by clients, judges, opposing counsel, policy makers, and others. As you develop and fine tune your intentionality muscles, I also want you to be strategic about your self-care practices: eating nutritiously, moving your body, and prioritizing quality rest.

A few words about self-care are warranted here.

The "self-care" industry has burgeoned into a multi-billion-dollar industry, ranging in products and services from candles, wearable devices (i.e., Fitbits, Oura rings), essential oils, massage services, meditation apps, supplements and much more. But the antidote to burnout cannot be a trip to the nail salon. If it were as simple as changing one's nail color or buying the hottest gadget (i.e., retail "therapy"), I doubt that the World Health Organization would recognize burnout as a significant issue.

In many ways, the self-care movement has taken center stage as individuals, families, communities, and companies grapple with what life looks like after COVID-19. Hollow prescriptions to "take time for yourself," "practice self-care," and "be kind to yourself," do not capture the essence of what it means to prioritize you. When I refer to self-care, I am not describing a once-in-a-blue-moon event or activity.

Do we have the entire self-care analysis wrong? That is, instead of focusing on one-time, episodic, feel-good practices, would we be better served sharpening longer-term, sustainable practices that truly invigorate us? My hypothesis is, yes. Knowing that self-care is foundational, not cosmetic, I often remind myself of the following:

- Self-care is therapy.
- Self-care is a spiritual practice.
- Self-care is setting healthy boundaries.
- Self-care can be free.
- Self-care is not self-indulgent.
- Self-care is sometimes an unapologetic "no," with zero follow-ups or explanation.
- Self-care is sometimes a thankful "yes."
- Self-care is sustainable.
- Self-care is not earned.
- Self-care is preventative.
- Self-care is a ritual.
- Self-care is scheduled.
- Self-care is service to others.
- Self-care is doing less.

Finally, self-care does not lead to regret. Yes, unplugging to watch a movie or your favorite TV show is one way to decompress. However, binge watching an entire series on Net-flix and avoiding studying and going to bed late is something you may regret the next day. Similarly, indulging in food that you know isn't good for you, is not self-care, especially if the purpose is to numb emotions that may need your attention.

Instead of asking, "Have I worked hard enough to deserve to rest?", I've started asking, "Have I rested enough to do my most loving and meaningful work?"

—Nicola Jane Hobbs

Control How You Show Up

If you value being in control, 1L year may be unsettling. During your first year, you cannot choose your classes, your professors, or the students in your section. As much as you would prefer to orchestrate these variables to your liking, you won't be able to. The foundational courses have already been selected—constitutional law, property, torts, contracts, criminal law, civil procedure, and legal research, and writing. It's a tough pill to swallow, knowing that you won't be able to call the shots regarding many aspects of 1L year. Ready for the good news? You have absolute control over how you show up to greet the challenges ahead. You are in command over more than you think, including the following:

- Your thoughts
- Your speech
- Your self-talk
- Your gratitude practice
- Your response to adversity
- Your perspective
- Your effort
- Your beliefs
- Your priorities
- Your work ethic
- Your habits

- How often you exercise
- How often you say "thank you"
- How often you take risks
- How much time you spend worrying
- How often you dwell on the past
- Whether you try again after a setback
- Who you surround yourself with (people who drain your energy or fill you up)
- Who you follow on social media (and whether you choose to be on social media during 1L year)
- Whether you multitask
- When you ask for help
- Whether you ask for help
- Who you ask for help
- With whom you share your time and energy

Return to this list often. Memorize controllables from this list. Ask yourself, "What can I control in this moment?" Not tomorrow. Not next week. Not next semester. Not after graduation. Right now. Search for opportunities to exercise control—this will enhance your confidence and create opportunities to exercise personal agency. For example, control where you prepare for class. It doesn't have to be the law library unless that's your preference. If being surrounded by stressed out, sleep-deprived, over-caffeinated, malnourished law students congregated in the library frays your nerves, explore other study spaces. Choose an environment that makes you feel at ease and receptive to learning. Experiment with other schools on campus such as the business, medical, engineering, or public health schools. Find a place with the perfect level of stimuli, whether it's a coffee shop, a quiet restaurant, a park, or the comfort of your own home. Action creates momentum, so make a decision. Acting on the choices you do have, even seemingly small ones, can enhance your overall wellbeing.

Take Control Of The Socratic Method By Being Prepared

For many first-year law students, nothing evokes more fear than the Socratic method. In this hallmark teaching style, professors ask questions during class to test students' understanding of concepts from the cases they read. Students must use a process called "issue spotting" to identify legal issues in real time as the professor adds new facts or hypotheticals to the case being discussed. This question-and-answer-based exchange is designed to clarify legal principles and crystallize black letter law.[24] The Socratic method requires students to publicly demonstrate their abilities and think on their feet. This can be terrifying for the most skilled and prepared student, and a potential disaster for those who did not complete the assigned reading.

The intensity of Socratic dialogues can vary dramatically depending on the professor. Some instructors solicit volunteers, and others "cold call" students without giving them advance notice of when they will be in the hot seat. Some professors tell individuals or groups of students in advance that they will be responsible for leading the discussion. One of my professors called on students alphabetically and another questioned students row by row. Based on the professor's preference (and the size of the class), when it's your turn, you may answer a single question, such as "What is the holding of the case?," or you may be "on call" for the entire class.

So, how can you control the controllables as it relates to the Socratic method? Understanding your professors' system and the types of questions they tend to ask will help you prepare for class. You may observe, for example, that your professor focuses on the nuts and bolts of the case—the

---

[24] Black letter law refers to legal principles that are well established and generally not subject to dispute. It is often the *application* of black letter law that leads to litigation.

parties' respective arguments, the legal issues to be decided, the holding of the case, and the reasoning of any concurring or dissenting opinions. Other professors may gravitate toward extra legal questions: What are the consequences of the decision? Does the ruling incentivize the right conduct? What are the public policy implications of deciding the case one way or another? Did the court "get it right"?

Conducted properly, the Socratic method will guide students' thinking and lead to an understanding of legal principles. Facilitating a Socratic dialogue is a skill, and some professors cannot navigate the questioning without lowering students' self-esteem. That's unfortunate, but again, we are focused only on what *we* can control.

I'll never forget my first encounter with the Socratic method. A week into one of my first year classes, my professor introduced a case by reviewing its procedural posture. The procedural posture describes the history of the case, i.e., what happened at the trial court level? What claims were adjudicated? What claims are being appealed? I was prepared for class. I had read the case the night before and outlined the decision carefully. The professor called on me to begin the Socratic dialogue.

With sweaty palms and a racing heart, I stumbled through the 30-minute barrage of questioning. All eyes were on me as I talked through the case in a classroom full of strangers. I *knew* the material. But the way the professor asked the questions felt like an attack—like I was fighting a battle she didn't want me to win.

My senses had gone haywire. I saw endless rows of students dispersed in the lecture hall and the professor standing in the center of the room. My throat constricted as I prepared to speak. I heard the persistent click-clack of students typing and then the anticipatory silence as the waiting audience grew impatient. As my grandmother would say, it was so quiet you could hear a mouse pee on cotton. I perceived this as an ominous sign of imminent defeat. In hindsight, it was unhelpful to view these physiological changes as a doomsday event. My increased heartbeat and sweaty palms did not mean that something was wrong. Because the Socratic method was a new way of learning, I substituted what I didn't know by making up stories about what was happening around me. My physiological reactions were unrelated to my abilities. Duh!

Arousal Reappraisal Can Help You Reframe Challenges

There was another way to interpret what was happening. If I grounded myself, I could have contextualized these changes and created a "best case" scenario of what my body was telling me. For example, sweating through my blouse and shaking in my seat could have signified that:

- I was being challenged
- I cared about doing a good job
- The task at hand was important to me
- I wanted to maximize the opportunity I'd been given
- I wanted to communicate what I had read the night before

In addition, I could have interpreted my physiological changes as my body preparing itself to meet the challenges ahead. Cognitive behavioral researchers call this technique "arousal reappraisal."

Before defining arousal reappraisal, let me ask you this: do you view stress as an invisible force propelling you toward success or as a hurdle you must overcome? Our beliefs about stress, whether we view it as a challenge to conquer or a threat leading to failure, can impact our bodies' response to it. If we think of stress arousal "as a tool that helps maximize performance,"[25] we are better positioned to develop superior

---

[25] Jeremy P. Jamieson, Wendy Berry Mendes & Matthew K. Nock, *Improving Acute Stress Responses: The Power of Reappraisal*, Current Directions in Psych. Sci., vol. 22, no. 1, at 51 (Feb. 2013).

outcomes, such as clearer thinking, the ability to see different perspectives, and enhanced creativity.

With arousal reappraisal, we can interpret our rapid breathing, for example, as a sign that our bodies are internally working (pumping blood and delivering oxygen) to prepare for success. If we incorrectly interpret our physical sensations, this "can interfere with performance in concrete ways, and become a negative self-fulfilling prophesy."[26] An increased heartbeat coupled with misinterpreting that change could lead to clouded judgment, inflexible thinking, and an inability to see multiple sides of an issue (required skills for law students and lawyers).

Our responses to stress, whether during a Socratic session or otherwise, can work to our advantage. Let's say you are "on call" in class, preparing to answer questions about a case. Do you tell yourself, "keep calm" or "get pumped up"?

Associate Professor of Business Administration at Harvard University, Alison Wood Brooks, has a theory about this. In 2014, Brooks published a remarkable study in the *Journal of Experimental Psychology*, debunking conventional wisdom that we should tell ourselves to relax before engaging in anxiety-producing activities.[27] Participants in the study were asked to perform tasks generally associated with angst, such as singing, public speaking, and solving math problems. Before engaging in these activities, participants were asked to say out loud one of the following: "I am calm," "I am excited," or no statement. Those who encouraged themselves to get pumped up (by saying "I am excited") performed better on the assigned tasks. Brooks explained that anxiety and excitement are both high-arousal emotions, meaning our bodies respond similarly to both states—e.g., increased respiration and higher cortisol. This "arousal congruency"

---

[26] McKinney, *Depression and Anxiety in Law Students*, at 16.

[27] A.W. Brooks, *Get Excited: Reappraising Pre-Performance Anxiety Excitement*, J. of Experimental Psych.: Gen., vol. 143(3), at 1144 (2014).

makes it easier to reappraise one "high-arousal emotion (anxiety) as another high-arousal emotion (excitement)."[28] Telling ourselves to be calm (which is a low-arousal emotion) is difficult when our body is already charged up. With simple statements like "I am excited" or "get excited," Brooks' research offers a powerful way to reframe potentially anxious situations (threat state) with excitement (opportunity state).

Back to the theme of this chapter: control the controllables. Volunteer in class. When you engage on your own terms, you get comfortable exercising your voice and build your confidence.

One final thought about the Socratic method: Most professors do not grade students' performance during the Socratic method. In other words, even if you bomb a dialogue, it will not come back to haunt you at the end of the semester. So, calm down—oops, I mean, get excited!

Embrace The "IRAC" Formula For Final Exams

After rigorously studying for an entire semester, assembling your outline (a document that synthesizes the cases, course themes, and black letter law), reviewing supplemental materials and attending lectures, you will likely have one opportunity to show your stuff each semester. Understandably, this can create anxiety.

Here's what you do: begin with the end in mind by preparing for final exams on the first day of class. Cramming the week before finals is akin to last-minute bar examination prep. There is simply too much information to digest. You will also miss nuances in the law if you try to bypass the process. There are no short cuts, remember?

It is beyond the scope of this book to provide an in-depth discussion on exam taking strategies, how to get on law review, how to land a judicial clerkship, or get the dream job (whatever that is for you) after law school. If you want more

---

[28] *Id.*

resources on these topics, these excellent books can help, including *1L of a Ride: A Well-traveled Professor's Roadmap to Success in the First Year of Law School* by Andrew McClurg, and *Law School Confidential: A Complete Guide to the Law School Experience: By Students, for Students* by Robert H. Miller. I don't want to overload you with technical aspects of outlining and taking exams, but I will offer general tips on exam strategies if this is the only law school prep book you read.

As a primer on exam taking strategies, here are the basics: most law school exams involve a written fact pattern with legal problems to "issue spot." On exams, professors will not ask you to regurgitate legal rules or answer specific questions about the cases you read during the semester. You will not see questions like "what is a tort?" or "what did the court hold in *International Shoe v. Washington?*"

There is a formula, an organizational framework, in structuring your exam responses. The two most common formulas are IRAC (issue, rule, application, or conclusion) or CRAC (conclusion, rule, application, conclusion). Thinking like a lawyer involves effective issue spotting, distilling complicated information, and offering clear conclusions or recommendations.

Issue spotting means identifying and analyzing the problems referenced in the fact pattern. Look for issues big and small, procedural and substantive. Procedural issues involve questions such as whether a claim has been brought within the statute of limitations or whether a party has exhausted their administrative remedies. Or the issues can be substantive—e.g., did Party A breach the contract or is Party B liable for tortious interference.

IRAC is incredibly versatile—it is the framework for many written deliverables.

Clerking for a judge? Writing bench memos and drafting legal opinions require clerks to understand the law, the parties' arguments, and identify issues before making recommendations to their judge.

Working in private practice? When preparing legal memoranda and emails to clients, you must frequently issue spot to properly advise your client. Conducting legal research? Legal briefs are nothing more than a persuasive issue spotting exercise.

Preparing for trial, arbitration, or an administrative proceeding? Crafting direct and cross examination questions requires you to firmly grasp the issues so that you can elicit testimony to advance your client's position and convince your audience that you should win.

Law school exam hypotheticals are often presented as narratives (sometimes several pages long), and you should pay close attention to every detail your professor includes. For example, a seemingly innocuous element, like the date of an accident, could apply to a statute of limitations issue. Every detail can be meaningful.

The professor may intentionally omit certain facts from the hypothetical too. In that case, you may need to make assumptions to support your conclusions by asking, "what missing information would help me comprehensively answer the questions?" For instance, you may write on a contracts exam, "the facts do not indicate whether Ms. Turner expressly accepted the offer presented to her. Accordingly, the enforceability of the contract at issue depends on whether Ms. Turner implicitly accepted the terms. If a court determines that Ms. Turner's actions demonstrated her assent to the bargain (even without specifically stating so), acceptance is valid here."

After you untangle the web of facts and correctly identify the issues, the next step is to apply the correct legal principles. Even if you argue both sides of an issue or provide the pros and cons of pursuing one path instead of another, if the professor asks you to reach a conclusion (i.e., is the defendant liable) or make a recommendation (i.e., how should the court rule), respond definitively to the prompt. In other words, answer the question asked. Using IRAC, an outline of a contracts exam answer may look something like this.

- *Issue*: The issue is whether the oral contract between buyer and seller is enforceable under New York law.

- *Rule*: The Statute of Frauds requires that contracts for the sale of goods in the amount of $500 or more must be in writing.

- *Application*: In this case, the parties entered into an oral contract on June 30, 2012. The seller agreed to provide 100 cases of water to buyer for the total amount of $650. The parties' oral agreement was not memorialized.

- *Conclusion*: Because the Statute of Frauds requires *written* contracts for the sale of goods in the amount of $500 or more, the oral agreement between buyer and seller is unenforceable.

Yes, I know this looks boring and robotic. That's intentional. Professors are not looking for flowery prose or legal fluff in your exam responses. Address the issues and move on to the next question. Law school exams are mechanical, and once you learn the formula, you can organize your thoughts into a stellar exam response.

Another word of caution: you are not meant to get everything "right" on an exam. Sometimes, the "right" answer doesn't exist. The objective is to show your professor your thought process in a logical, organized way.

Analyze each issue slowly and methodically. Issue. Rule. Application. Conclusion. That's the formula for writing a successful law school exam.

Read With A Purpose

Cultivate active reading skills now. Reading in massive quantities comes with the territory of being a law student. This is

just the beginning. No matter what area of law you eventual-
ly practice, you will be paid to read for a living. Establishing
first-rate reading habits while in law school, will serve you
well as an attorney. As you engage with the assigned reading
for your classes, you can ask yourself questions along the
way:

- Can I summarize the case in a way my non-lawyer
  friends would understand the principles? Do I have
  any questions about the material?

- What's making sense? If it took me longer to read the
  material than the time I allotted, why is that true?

- Can I predict how the case will come out?

- Do I agree with the majority's opinion? The concur-
  rence? The dissent? Why?

- If I were the lawyer arguing the case, would I have
  structured my arguments the same way?

- How does this case fit into the larger context of what
  I am learning? In other words, where does this fall in
  the syllabus?

- How might my professor test my knowledge and understanding of the legal principles in this case?

You must have energy to read and digest information effectively. In Ruth Ann McKinney's article, "Reading Like a
Lawyer: Time-Saving Strategies for Reading Like an Expert,"
she describes law school reading as an active process, where
students and the text are engaged in conversation with one
another.[29] Sometimes, this exercise requires wrestling with
complex written texts in a way you have never done. If you
lack the necessary oomph to interact with the assigned reading, take a break or start a task that does not require as much
mental rigor.

---

[29] Ruth Ann McKinney, "Reading Like A Lawyer: Time-Saving Strategies For Reading Law Like An Expert" (2d ed. 2012) 61.

Create A Closing Ritual

The legal profession is infused with rituals. Before delivering an opening statement during an oral argument, attorneys often start their presentation saying, "May it please the Court." To mark the conclusion of presenting their case, you will hear "the plaintiff [or defense] rests their case."

As mentioned above, during law school, it may feel like there is always more to do. Your daily task list can feel endless—more cases to read and brief, more outlines to draft, more practice exams to take, more applications to send to prospective employers, and more flash cards to review. If you let it, law school can expand to fill every second of every day.

One way to mark the end of your day is to implement a closing ritual. This practice helps your body and mind sense what "done" looks and feels like. A closing ritual signals to your brain that you have finished and can transition to a state of rest. My closing ritual involves three steps.

1. Acknowledge What I Have Accomplished For The Day

When I skip this, it is easy for me to say things like "I didn't even scratch the surface of my to-do list. Look at how many things are still looming." But when I take the time to actually reflect on my day, I can always find at least one accomplishment (even if it's the success of *starting* a project, or on rare occasions *thinking* about *starting* a project). Drawing attention to this, evokes gratitude, which creates a positive foundation for the following day.

2. Physically Signify That The Work Is Done

At the end of a workday, my "switch off gesture" involves closing my laptop followed by a short pause that initiates my process of disconnection. Other "switch off gestures" can include closing your case book, silencing the notifications on your phone until the next morning, turning off your desk lamp, or shutting your planner. You may already instinctively do some of these activities, but when you bring awareness to them, it can symbolize that it is time to unplug.

3. Manifest Completing An Important Task For The Following Day

The last step of my closing ritual is to visualize accomplishing a meaningful task on my to-list for the following day. This gives me a head start on the project and allows my subconscious time to work the issue before I sit down to problem solve.

In this chapter, we discussed what can make the uncharted territory of law school unnerving. Now that you have specific tools to address the difficult aspects of law school, including the Socratic method, and final exams, you are better equipped to show up even when the task at hand is demanding. Although some aspects of law school are beyond your control, focus on what you can direct.

Solo Sidebar

Revisit the definitions of self-care referenced earlier in this chapter. To take this a step further, I invite you to write down your self-care plan. There are many professional and life transitions that we would not dare to start without first having a plan in place. Executives create business, financial, and marketing plans. Schools and employers have fire escape plans. Expectant parents often have birth plans to prepare for labor. These blueprints help individuals and companies thoughtfully consider desired outcomes and plan for contingencies. The same intensity should apply when preparing to elevate our well-being.

Here are some things to consider as you develop a personalized self-care roadmap. The objective is to determine what *you* need to experience wholeness along the following spectrums.

Physical Wellbeing

- Are you getting adequate sleep? If not, what changes do you need to make?
- Are you eating a well-balanced diet? If not, how can you incorporate more fruit, fresh vegetables, and water into your routine?
- Are you getting enough exercise? If not, how can you make physical activity enjoyable and a regular part of your life?

Emotional and Mental Wellbeing

- What boundaries do you need to establish to prioritize your emotional and mental wellbeing?
- Are there people or activities that you need to say no to?
- Are you striving for perfection or excellence?

Spiritual Wellbeing

- Are you engaging in fulfilling spiritual practices? Note that a spiritual practice does not necessarily need to involve religion—it is about connecting to and with something deeper than you.

Relational Wellbeing

- What are you doing to nurture your relationships?

For each category, identify your current practices and any new strategies you want to implement. Writing this down can help you immediately see the areas that need attention. One question to repeatedly come back to is, what is the best thing you can do right now for yourself?

Concluding Mindfulness Practice: The Full Body Scan

The full body scan is an excellent way to focus on your breath and bring awareness to your entire body. This scan can be done sitting, standing, or lying down, with your eyes open or closed.

To begin, get into a position that feels comfortable. Take a few breaths to warm up and get into a natural rhythm to observe your breath without manipulation—is it deep or shallow? Constrained or unrestricted? Try not to manipulate the breath at first. Instead, allow its natural cadence to flow freely.

As you scan slowly and deliberately, bring your attention to individual parts of your body, noticing whether there is tension, pain, aches, or any general discomfort. If you come to areas that need nourishment, on an inhale, imagine that you are sending your breath to that space, and on the exhale invite ease into that spot. If you encounter areas that are tense, ask yourself if there's a way to release or let go of some of the discomfort. If it helps to shake out a tight wrist, or roll out a shoulder, or self-massage the neck, by all means, attend to what your body needs in the moment. Move at your own pace.

Let's start the body scan by bringing awareness to the soles of your feet. Notice the parts of your body that are touching the chair, floor, or surface you are lying on. If sitting down or standing, observe the way in which your feet are contacting the floor. Are you barefoot? If not, notice the shoes you are wearing, the texture of your socks, whether the weight of your body is more concentrated in the heels or the toes. What sensations arise if you ground down further into the floor to create more stability?

Move from your feet to your ankles, flexing and pointing the toes, then rotating the ankles. On the next inhale, trace the breath along your shins, knees, and thighs. Observe how the chair or floor is supporting you. Bring your attention to your hips and pelvis; allow them to soften. Move to the low belly, releasing your abdominal muscles. Feel the belly and chest rise and fall as you cycle through your breaths. Drop your fingers, wrists, forearms, and shoulders down. Let gravity do the work.

Relax the muscles in your face. You may want to massage your jaw with the heels of your hands to release tension. Unclench your teeth. Invite gentleness into the area in between your eyebrows. If your default is a furrowed brow, smooth out that space by tracing your middle and index fingers from the center of your forehead to the outside of your eyebrows. While you are in the vicinity, give your temples some love by gently massaging them. To do so, place your thumbs on your jaw or cheekbones and use your fingertips to draw mini circles at your temples. There are more than forty muscles in the face alone, so as you scan the body, invite tenderness there.

After your full body scan is complete, settle in for a few moments of rest, noticing what, if anything, has changed in your body. What feels relieved, cared for, and maybe even free?

5

Speak Your Mind to Free Your Mind

When I put down what is not mine to carry, I am free.

—Octavia Faith Ann Raheem

What does it mean to be a historically underrepresented student in law school? Are there dynamics in the law school classroom that uniquely impact students with diverse backgrounds? If so, what are they?

Before going any further, let me start this chapter with an invitation: even if you do not identify as historically underrepresented, please continue reading as there is valuable information for everyone to consider. This chapter examines how race can show up in law school and provides a framework (called "mindful redirection") that will allow you to confront negative comments whether they are based on a protected class or simply discourteous.

Although historically underrepresented students may not experience overt discrimination in law school, they may encounter micro-aggressions, implicit bias, and other unwanted forces that amplify an already challenging landscape. If diverse students look around, will they see themselves represented in the teaching faculty, staff, and administrators? If not, this can send unintentional messages about inclusion and belonging. Concerns about inclusivity can even arise in institutions that champion diversity efforts.

Some of the legal themes presented during 1L year can involve race, gender, religion, and ethnicity. Although "the law" aims to be neutral, history is a sobering reminder that it often falls short. In fact, there are many examples of bias, inequality, and injustice that animate our legal system. Will professors connect textbook, black letter law to controversial contemporary social issues? In my view, a criminal law class is *not* truly a criminal law class without discussing the larger context and historical backdrops that remain relevant, and in some cases, are outcome determinative. Will professors minimize, whitewash, or ignore the reality that many of our institutions are fatally (and, in some cases, literally fatally) defective? Do students feel compelled to dilute their experiences at the intersection of race, for example, and the law to make these conversations more palatable to classmates and even professors? How do students decide when to speak up or remain silent? If students speak up and offer an opposing or contextualizing point of view, will they be perceived as divisive or unable to analyze the law "rationally"?

Perspectivelessness In Legal Education

Professor Kimberle' Williams Crenshaw—one of the founders of critical race theory—describes "perspectivelessness" in legal education as an assumption that the law is neutral and objective. In one example, Professor Crenshaw illustrates a dilemma involving an agent working for Immigration and Customs Enforcement (ICE). The question was whether the agent had reasonable cause to detain Latine passengers in a car. If a Latine law student is then called on in class to analyze the reasonableness of this encounter, there is a "tension created by the expectation of objectivity" and the possibility that this student may have real world experiences, personal or otherwise, with broader issues concerning citizenship status.[30]

According to Professor Crenshaw, there are at least two problems with a perspectivelessness or colorless approach to studying legal doctrines. It can force diverse students to "assume a stance that denies their own identity and requires

[30] Kimberle' Williams Crenshaw, "Toward a Race-Conscious Pedagogy in Legal Education," *National Black Law Journal,* 11, no. 1 (1988).

them to adopt an apparently objective stance as the given starting point of analysis."[31] If they venture outside of what it means to "think like a lawyer," they have seemingly failed the task at hand, which is to apply the law logically, reasonably, and unemotionally. As a result, students may minimize their experiential knowledge to demonstrate to the professor and other students that they can be rational, dispassionate legal thinkers. In this sense, they are asked to be perspectiveless.

Minority Testifying

The second problem Professor Crenshaw identifies is minority "testifying," where a student's racial identity is "unexpectedly dragged into the classroom by their instructor to illustrate a point or to provide the basis for a command performance of 'show and tell.'"[32] Although students with common traits may have shared experiences, one person cannot speak to the richness and complexity of the views, experiences, beliefs, and values of an entire group. In addition, being singled out in a classroom (or workplace) to discuss issues concerning race, for example, suggests that diverse students can only provide insight when the discussion concerns a protected characteristic. This is a dangerous, limiting assumption.

I remember two examples of race showing up in the classroom that mirror Professor Crenshaw's perspectiveless concept. During a criminal law class, we were discussing different levels of mens rea[33] in a case involving sexual assault—a crime allegedly perpetrated by a Black man. There were only a handful of Black students in the classroom to begin with, so I was immediately on edge, waiting to see how

---

[31] Kimberle' Williams Crenshaw, *Toward a Race-Conscious Pedagogy in Legal Education*, National Black Law Journal, 1988.

[32] *Id.*

[33] Mens rea refers to the state of mind that is necessary to convict a defendant of a specific crime. There are different levels of mens rea, such as negligently, recklessly, knowingly, and purposefully.

the discussion would unfold. When my Caucasian professor asked one of the two Black men in the class questions about the mens rea that should be imputed to the accused, I couldn't chalk that up to coincidence. Even if it wasn't deliberate, I interpreted my professor's decision to call on this specific Black student as a way of symbolically equating criminality with race. It was as if this student was actually on trial, being cross-examined by the professor, as she peppered him with questions (yes, using the Socratic method). I was enraged. I shut down for the remainder of the class, unable to concentrate on anything else. I kept replaying the dialogue hours after the class ended.

The weight of that session followed me home. It was a soreness invisible to others, but one I felt intensely. Before I could prepare for the next class, I needed to shed the baggage of that poorly handled exchange and did so by talking with a law school friend. I did not want to blow anything out of proportion, so I questioned whether I was justified feeling this way. Was I being too sensitive? Did anyone else in the classroom feel uncomfortable? (I later found out I wasn't the only one.) Could it have been a coincidence that the professor decided to call on *that* particular student for *that* specific case? Why couldn't I snap back into study mode? Asking and attempting to answer questions like this depleted my energy and stole valuable time away from studying.

Race regrettably showed up in the classroom again during an elective class as we discussed the First Amendment and whether certain hate speech could be constitutionally protected. In *Snyder v. Phelps*, a 2011 United States Supreme Court decision, members of the Westboro Baptist Church picketed the funeral of a U.S. Marine, who identified as gay and died in the Iraq War. Westboro Baptist Church believed the U.S. was becoming increasingly tolerant of homosexuality and led a protest, carrying horrific signs that read, "Thank God for Dead Soldiers" and "F*gs Doom Nations." Justice

Samuel Alito, in his dissenting opinion, described the hate-filled words of the picketers as a "vicious verbal assault."[34] The deceased Marine's family sued Westboro Baptist Church for intentional infliction of emotional distress, among other causes of action. The question at issue? Was the church's speech protected by the First Amendment? The Supreme Court said that it was protected by the First Amendment because the speech related to a public issue.

My Caucasian professor wanted to highlight other examples of hate-filled, injurious words. Then, she blurted out the N-word.

No warning.

No hesitation.

Out loud.

In front of the entire class.

And no, she didn't abbreviate it.

That word sucked the air out of the room. As a Black woman, was I supposed to ignore the historical origins of this word and its weaponization to harass, humiliate, and de-humanize people who look like me? Should I have tossed my personal indignation aside and pretended that using this word, even for illustrative purposes, was a proper starting point for a legal analysis?

Several students went to the professor's office hours after class and explained why her decision to use this word was appalling, despite her intentions to educate and, I'm assuming, be provocative in her approach. The professor apologized privately to the students who went to her office hours, and then publicly to the class the following session.

In the two examples shared above, I did not have a fancy framework or terminology like "perspectiveless" to describe what I felt. But I knew these were real moments of discomfort and alienation. Here's what I wish I had known in those queasy situations.

---

[34] *Snyder v. Phelps*, 562 U.S. 443, 463 (2011).

- The squeamish moments are full of opportunity. If an issue is framed too narrowly, you have an opening to showcase how well you can apply the law to the facts *and* highlight your legal dexterity in taking different, perhaps broader viewpoints. You can challenge assumptions and frameworks that professors may present as a given.

- Your unique attributes (and we all have them) are gifts to be embraced. Bringing what makes you special into the conversation will make you a better lawyer. Your experiential knowledge is relevant, needed, and valuable. When it comes down to it, lawyers are problem solvers, and the best attorneys seize opportunities to see multiple angles. How is my adversary viewing this case? What is the plaintiff's or defendant's perspective? How will the judge see the dispute? What arguments will resonate with the jury? If we pursue an alternative dispute mechanism, such as mediation or arbitration, how will the neutral third party view the facts? All in all, weaving in, out, around, and through these different lenses will make you a stronger advocate.

If professors, colleagues, or clients create a false tension between bringing a diverse perspective into the conversation and "thinking like a lawyer," remember that you do not have to choose. It's not one or the other. And it may be up to you to challenge the very questions that are asked so that a richer discussion can take place and better solutions achieved.

Mindful Redirection Will Help You Show Up And Shine

In the increasingly divisive world in which we live, the question emerges, how do we navigate unevenness, prejudice, insensitivity, or anything that makes us uncomfortable? What's the game plan? Thankfully, we have options, including direct confrontation, remaining silent, and tactfully addressing the concern in the moment if we so choose.

Direct confrontation can be daunting and depending on the circumstances, intimidating. Truth be told, we may not know what to say when things catch us off guard, leaving us scratching our heads asking, "Did she really just say that?" How many times have you left a conversation thinking, "I wish I had said [fill in the blank with the greatest comeback ever]"?

Silence is appealing in some situations. As a protective mechanism, we may hold back, out of fear that speaking up could damage relationships or lead to retaliation (such as getting fired from a job or not being promoted). We may also choose silence to avoid reactions that will make us look fragile, something seemingly antithetical to a zealous, fight-to-the-death advocate. Silence may be attractive if there are personal and professional consequences at stake, particularly when unequal power structures exist. No one wants to be branded a complainer, a troublemaker, or too sensitive. But unequal power structures do not mean you are powerless. You have a right to be treated with dignity, and if someone infringes or threatens to infringe on this right, their behavior should not continue unchallenged.

But silence can also be costly. When we choose this path, we can implicitly condone the offensive behavior and leave the door open for unwelcome comments to continue or intensify. There's also a risk that silence will become our default response. If we don't practice speaking up, our voice may atrophy, weakening one of the most powerful assets in our protective toolkit. Most of us believe that when it counts, when it truly matters, we will courageously speak truth to power (or, in some cases, truth to BS)—whether that means standing up for ourselves or for others who experience unfairness. But when real life happens—when our feet are held to the fire—we may not act in the heroic way we envisioned.

There may be a disconnect between how we see ourselves and how we actually respond. When we don't speak up (and later wish we had), we can't help but replay the scene in our mind, torturing ourselves about what we could have or should have said. Ruminations can lead to obsessive thinking, which can slash our productivity, emotional well-being, and confidence.

Don't get me wrong, sometimes, exercising restraint is the wiser course. In the proper context, intentionally choosing silence or knowing when to simply walk away is powerful. I am not advocating that you speak up in *every* situation without carefully considering the circumstances. My goal is to highlight that your "confrontation arsenal" can hold more than silence, avoidance, cursing someone out, or bursting into tears. These responses may have their place, but they are not the only options.

Defining Mindful Redirection

There's an alternative—an approach I call *mindful redirection*—using a verbal response to immediately shift comments that leave you feeling minimized, written off, inferior, depleted, or devalued. Mindful redirection does not require a lengthy dissertation accompanied by facts and figures to effectively communicate how you want to be treated. It can be as simple as one or two words, all designed to release the weight of comments you were never intended to bear. Mindful redirection encourages you to make, what authors Marcel Zeelenberg and Nannie K. De Vries call, "regret-minimizing choices."[35] Before leaving a conversation, meeting, or encounter, ask yourself, *"If I choose silence in this moment, will I regret this decision later"*? If the answer is yes, mindful redirection may be valuable to explore.

---

[35] Marcel Zeelenberg, Jane Beattie, Joop Van Der Pligt & Nannie K. De Vries, *Consequences of Regret Aversion: Effects of Expected Feedback on Risky Decision Making*, Org. Behavior & Human Decision Processes, vol. 65, no. 2, at 148–58 (Feb. 1996).

Mindful Redirection In Action

Here's one example of mindful redirection in action. When I was a mid-level associate at a law firm, I attended a court conference with a senior attorney—let's call him Jeremy. The purpose of the conference was to meet with the judge to set discovery deadlines and discuss the parties' respective positions in the litigation. There was a large wood conference table in the front of the courtroom. The judge sat on one side of the table, and there were three chairs on the opposite side for the attorneys. In this case, two lawyers represented the plaintiffs, and Jeremy and I represented the defendant.

Three chairs. Four attorneys.

While we waited in the gallery, Jeremy knew someone would be left standing in this *a cappella* game of courtroom musical chairs. So, before the judge called our case, Jeremy leaned over and whispered to me, "Since there are only three chairs at the table, why don't you hang back in the gallery. I'll update you after we talk to the judge." Wanting to be agreeable, I said, "Sure, no problem."

As I continued to mull over Jeremy's request while sitting in the gallery, I grew agitated, first with Jeremy and then with myself. I wanted to hear the judge's perspective first-hand. I envisioned going home and calling my parents with frustration because Jeremy asked me to wait in the gallery of the courtroom while the "real attorneys" (who happened to be white men) conferred with the judge. In the monologue I imagined later delivering, I was indignant about traveling on the subway in the freezing cold to get to the courthouse first thing in the morning, all to be told to "hang out" in the gallery.

I do not believe race or gender motivated Jeremy's request (in fact, Jeremy was one of my biggest supporters and mentors at the firm). Maybe it was because I was the most junior person on the team or because he wanted a quick fix to the seating shortage. Whatever the reason, it did not sit well with me, and I anticipated the regret of remaining silent as I watched the scene play out in real time.

Then, it hit me, like a judge banging her gavel that I still had time to speak up. Several seconds had passed since my initial response of "Sure, no problem." Just as matter-of-factly as Jeremy made his request, I matter-of-factly told him my solution: "Let's ask the bailiff to find another chair and bring it to the table. There's enough room for a fourth chair." He responded, "Of course," still not recognizing that, had I complied with the initial request, I would have unnecessarily sacrificed a literal seat at the table.

Instead of leaving the courtroom that day feeling suffocated by my own silence, like I wasn't part of the team, or that I lacked control, I sashayed back to the office feeling like a giant. I would have been incredibly disappointed had I not spoken up in the moment. I had no regrets that day.

In the sections that follow, we will explore ways to implement mindful redirection by inviting curiosity, making it clear when certain behaviors should stop, and repeating the problematic comment back to the speaker to diffuse its impact.

Invite Curiosity

You can use mindful redirection by asking questions to shift or disrupt the flow of conversations. The questions and comments below are designed to invite curiosity.

- "What information are you basing that on?"[36]
- "I'm confused by what you said. Can you please clarify?"
- "Do you really feel that way?"
- "What are you implying by that?"
- "What did you mean by that [comment, remark, question]?"
- "Say more about that."

[36] Joan Williams, *How to Respond to an Offensive Comment at Work*, Harvard Business Review, https://hbr.org/2017/02/how-to-respond-to-an-offensive-comment-at-work?ab=at_articlepage_relatedarticles_horizontal_slot2 (Feb. 8, 2017).

- "Help me understand where you are coming from in [saying, assuming, stating] _____."
- "Walk me through your thought process in making that claim."
- "Let's break that down."
- "You seem to be assuming _____. Do I understand that correctly?"
- "What leads you to say that?"
- "Can you give me an example?"

Nip It In A Bud

You may decide to squash the behavior or more directly communicate how the comment landed. Consider the following nip-it-in-a-bud statements:

- "That's not okay with me."
- "I know it wasn't your intent, but that comment made me uncomfortable."[37]
- "That's offensive. Please don't say that again around me."
- "Cut it out."
- "What you just said is harmful."
- "That was hurtful."
- "I know you're not [sexist, racist, homophobic, xenophobic, etc.], so I'm surprised to hear you say that."
- "I don't think [that joke, comment, etc.] is funny."
- "I disagree."
- "That's enough."
- "Yuck—that comment left a bad taste in my mouth."

Verbal Replay

Another way to implement mindful redirection is to repeat what has been said or ask the person to repeat the statement out loud. This exercise of "verbal replay" allows the speaker to hear their own words out loud. If the playback does not

---

[37] *Id.*

make the speaker clarify their statement, that's okay too. The point is—you don't want other people's words saddling you. Here are several verbal replay examples:

- "Did you really just say _____?"
- "Can you repeat that?"
- "Give me a second. I need to process what you just said, which if I heard it correctly is _____."
- "I hear you saying [repeat the comment]. Is that right?"
- "Run that by me again."

And if you don't know what to say or if none of these suggestions fit the scenario, your default response can be: "That comment deserves a response. This is something we should discuss later."

Allies Are Only Part Of The Answer

From the lists above, identify the phrases that feel natural to you and practice saying them out loud, maybe in front of a mirror. When (not if) the time comes for you to speak up, I want you to have a repertoire of responses to actively participate in your own empowerment. Mindful redirection frees you from relying on someone else's willingness to speak on your behalf. Although allies are important, it is too risky to consistently loan our voice to someone else. Allies may choose silence themselves, whether paralyzed by their own fear or concerns about retaliation. Allies who do speak up for you may be motivated by external praise or because they see you as incapable. I want you to participate in your own well-being, and as often as you can, be your own advocate. Mindful redirection allows you to do just that.

We should assume the best of people, not that they intended to make us feel inferior. After all, we don't know their true feelings, intentions, or perspectives—only our own. We can give people the benefit of the doubt *and* protect ourselves from disaffirming experiences. These options are not mutually exclusive. What I like about mindful redirection is that it allows us to maintain our civility and speak up for ourselves. Cassandra Dahnke and Tomas Spath, co-founders of the Institute for Civility in Government, define civility as follows:

> Civility is claiming and caring for one's identity, needs and beliefs without degrading someone else's in the process... [Civility] is about disagreeing without disrespect, seeking common ground as a starting point for dialogue about differences, listening past one's preconceptions, and teaching others to do the same. Civility is the hard work of staying present even with those with whom we have deep-rooted and fierce disagreements. It is political in the sense that it is a necessary prerequisite for civic action. But it is political, too, in the sense that it is about negotiating interpersonal power such that everyone's voice is heard, and nobody's is ignored.[38]

What is the goal of mindful redirection? To uncover biases individuals may harbor and change their hearts and minds? To put people in their place? Not at all. Mindful redirection is about you. If people change their behaviors, that's great, but the true aim is to unleash your resonant voice. You can control what you internalize, recognizing that you do not have to absorb the impact of a snide or uninformed comment. Get that weight immediately off your shoulders. It's not meant for you.

Solo Sidebar

1. What additional words, phrases, and questions can you add to the mindful redirection framework?

[38] Tomas Spath & Cassandra Dahnke, *What is Civility?*, Institute for Civility in Government, https://www.instituteforcivility.org/who-we-are/what-is-civility/.

2. Are there situations where you tend to remain silent? For the circumstances that come to mind, consider whether silence in those moments is "regret minimizing."

Concluding Mindfulness Practice: Music Meditation

Listening to music can usher us to calming or energetic states. Familiar songs can spark powerful memories, transport us back to special moments, and allow the emotions associated with those moments to reemerge.

In this exercise, select a meditation song and then block off two to five minutes of uninterrupted time to listen. You can choose a relaxing, slow-paced song to practice synchronizing your breath to the rhythm. But if you prefer an upbeat, invigorating melody to get pumped up, give it a try—remember this is all about what you need. You can even experiment with ambient or nature sounds and instrumental music. Anything will work!

To begin the exercise, find a comfortable seated position and settle in. Relax your neck and shoulders. If you are in public, insert your earbuds and mindfully listen to one of your favorite songs or find a new tune to explore. From start to finish, while intentionally breathing, listen, really *listen* to the song. Observe the lyrics, the rhythm, the instruments. If your environment permits, close your eyes so that you can fully immerse yourself in the song, and perhaps discover something you have never noticed.

6

CONCENTRATE ON THE MAGNIFICENT PATH IN FRONT OF YOU

Comparison is the thief of joy.

—Theodore Roosevelt

Law school heightens an innate tendency to compare ourselves to others. Before you start measuring yourself against other students, this chapter cautions against comparisons, introduces the Dunning-Kruger effect, which suggests that people who *appear* to know it all may actually be clueless, and provides methods to respond to comparison urges.

Comparison-driven thoughts and behaviors can wreak unnecessary havoc during law school. Whether it's what psychologists call a *downward comparison* (comparing yourself to someone you believe is worse off) or an *upward comparison* (comparing yourself to someone you perceive as better off), both are unproductive detours that diminish your gratitude practice.

With downward comparisons, instead of gratitude, we focus on those we perceive to have less. This can evoke feelings of superiority as we measure our abilities against those who appear to have fewer skills or resources. An example of a downward comparison is being thankful for performing better in class than someone who painfully stumbled through a Socratic session. In the short term, a downward comparison may boost our confidence and self-esteem, but the feeling is not sustainable. True gratitude does not involve comparisons. It's about appreciating our circumstances, as they exist.

With upward comparisons, instead of gratitude, our attention is redirected to people who appear to be living their best lives. You know what this looks like. These folks seem to visit exotic destinations every other weekend. They seem to study very little yet ace their exams. Inevitably, upward comparisons can create feelings of inadequacy—an artificial belief that we need more money, time, friends, vacations, or whatever "it" is to be fulfilled.

I love this definition of comparison from Brene' Brown. In her book, *Atlas of the Heart*, Brown says that comparison "is the crush of conformity from one side and competition from the other—it's trying to simultaneously fit in and stand out. Comparison says, 'Be like everyone else, but better.'"[39] This definition is particularly fitting in law school because students want to conform to some degree, and outperform their counterparts. For example, every law student wants to graduate from law school (blend in), but also graduate with honors (stand out).

Comparisons make you feel superior or inferior.
Neither serves a useful purpose.

—Jane Travis

Here's the problem. When we cede to comparison-driven thoughts in law school, we suffocate our gratitude practice because we are no longer in the moment, but rather creating narratives about what other students are doing (or not doing). Envy, insecurity, discouragement, and self-pity result from playing the comparison game. As we discussed in chapter 2, gratitude gives us a transformative lens to see that we have everything we need to flourish. In comparison to no one.

You alone are enough. You have nothing to prove to anybody.

—Maya Angelou

Because comparison fuels competition and chills creativity, intentionally focus on the unique path in front of you.

---

[39] Brené Brown, *Atlas of the Heart: Mapping Meaningful Connection and the Language of Human Experience* (New York: Random House, 2021) 22-23.

Granted, this may be difficult in an environment that lacks consistent feedback and where grades seem to be valued above all else. You are no stranger to competition. You persevered to get into law school, and it may feel like you're back in the arena once again, competing against your fellow 1Ls. This time, the extrinsic prizes include a high class rank, invitations to participate on law journals, clerking for state or federal judges, participating in coveted legal clinics, and getting offers to work at "prestigious" companies, law firms, or non-profits.

Seeking external confirmation by comparing yourself to others can make you question your competence and infuse doubt into every decision you make. Am I studying enough? Am I networking enough? Did I join the right extracurriculars? Have I started outlining at the right time? Am I learning how to "think like a lawyer" (and learning to do so fast enough)? Do I know how to issue spot? Am I using the IRAC method properly? Am I attending office hours frequently enough? Iyanla Vanzant, inspirational speaker and lawyer, went so far to say that "[c]omparison is an act of violence against the self."

Comparisons are rarely based on accurate information. They are superficial at best, and at worst, they are littered with assumptions and misinformation. In law school, for example, some students intentionally misrepresent the amount of time they spend preparing for class. If you compare yourself to the person who *claims* they spent 15 hours outlining the day before, you may feel pressure to ramp up your study time even if you've accomplished what you need to for the day. The person you are measuring yourself against may work more slowly than you. Or they may spend more time in the library because they incessantly check their phone while attempting to study.

On the other hand, if you hear that someone is studying less than you, this may give you false confidence. That is risky too. Get your work done by constructing an internal barometer to monitor your progress.

> *If you pay attention to your ranking and comparison to others, you are competing with others. If you ignore them, you can aim for the stars.*

—Khang Kijarro Nguyen

Introducing…The Law School Gunner

Inspired by an actual conversation between two law students.

Law Student 1: I'm so tired. I stayed up working until one a.m. this morning.

Law Student 2: Really? You are more well rested that I am. I pulled an all-nighter, working on an article for law review.

Law Student 1: Wow, an all-nighter? That's awful. I'm trying to get ahead with my outlining. So far, my contracts outline is complete. One down; three more to go!

Law Student 2: Well, all four of my outlines have been done for weeks. I'm coasting right now.

Law Student 1: Good for you. I need to start taking practice exams. As soon as my outlines are done, that's next on my list.

Law Student 2: I've already taken two timed practice tests and reviewed them with my professors to get feedback. I'm actually taking a quick weekend trip to Bora Bora—it feels incredible to be ahead.

The temptation to compare is strongest when confronted with the law school one-upper or "gunner." People say that if you don't know who the gunner is, look in the mirror because you may be that person. These students love to hear their own voice and tend to hijack in-class discussions. Think of gunners as more sophisticated and more competitive versions of the teacher's pet from middle school. Like other law school challenges, you can handle gunners in several ways.

You can ignore them, recognizing that the students who actually know what's going on are not necessarily the most vocal in class. Social psychologists David Dunning and Justin Kruger describe a cognitive bias where less competent people sometimes "grossly overestimate their skills and abilities" without realizing it.[40] In other words, "[p]eople don't know what they don't know."[41] This cognitive bias, called the Dunning-Kruger effect, posits that people who *appear* as though they know it all are probably the least informed.[42] My point is, gunners could be masking their cluelessness.

Responding To Comparison-Driven Thoughts

I won't waste time asking you to "stop comparing yourself to others." This is not realistic. Silencing comparisons may be impossible, but we can be aware of when we do it, how it makes us feel, and whether we can benefit from these feelings. In other words, how can we positively respond to comparison impulses? Can we learn something from the comparison? Does it motivate us to be better versions of ourselves? Is there a useful approach to studying that we may want to incorporate based on observing others? By all means, experiment with methods that resonate with you and complement your learning style.

Don't be afraid to establish your own guideposts as they relate to your study habits. Before opening your casebook to read, set discrete goals and stop working (or take a well-deserved break) when you cross specific tasks off your to-do list. Setting boundaries in this way frees you to say "enough" after you have accomplished your goal.

It is a privilege to spend three years surrounded by other accomplished students. But remember, you are one of them!

---

[40] Justin Kruger and David Dunning, *Unskilled and Unaware of It: How Difficulties in Recognizing One's Incompetence Lead to Inflated Self-Assessments*, J. of Personality & Soc. Psych., vol. 77, no. 6., at 1121–34 (2000).

[41] *Id.*

[42] *Id.*

Don't let upward or downward comparisons let amnesia set in, making you forget the value you bring to the table. Eyes forward. Focus on your own progress. Set personal metrics. Stay the course.

Solo Sidebar

1. What are three unique qualities and strengths you possess that cannot be compared to others?

2. What can you learn from the comparison?

3. Does the comparison stir up something good in you?

4. Is the comparison weighing you down or propelling you forward?

5. What are three healthy boundaries you can set to minimize exposure to comparison triggers?

6. How are you progressing in comparison to the metrics you have set for *yourself*?

Concluding Mindfulness Practice: Seated or Standing Cat-Cow

This practice can be done sitting or standing. Begin by firmly planting your feet on the floor. Lengthen your spine and engage your core. Lift your arms so that they take the shape of a goal post, with your elbows bent 90 degrees and palms facing one another. As you inhale slightly lift the chest, arch the back, and tilt the head back slightly to stretch the throat. As you exhale, bring your elbows together to touch while contracting and rounding the spine so that it takes a "C" shape. With every inhale, the arms expand back to the side in the goal post formation, and the exhale brings the elbows together. Remember to connect your breath to the movements.

7

Cross-Examine Unproductive Thoughts

You can't go back and change the beginning, but you can start where you are and change the ending.

—C.S. Lewis

Michael Phelps, the most decorated Olympian of all time, is a master visualizer. Interestingly, Phelps did not just visualize swimming the perfect race. In training, he also envisioned how he would respond if things did not go as planned. This training and visualization practice allowed Phelps to win a gold medal and set a world record swimming the 200m butterfly at the Beijing Olympics in 2008. All this, despite not being able to see for the last 75m when water filled up his goggles. He had visualized this too.

The first year of law school requires planning and being flexible when circumstances demand it. As you plan for success, I also want you to consider what might deter you from reaching your goals. Those distractions could involve checking social media or email when you are supposed to be studying. Engaging in productive procrastination can be just as distracting. Yes, cleaning your apartment and deep conditioning your hair are important (please don't neglect your personal hygiene in law school!), but stay laser focused on the important tasks at hand. Like Phelps' visualization exercises, sometimes protecting your goals involves thinking about what could go wrong—and then creating a strategy to overcome the challenge.

This chapter provides a framework to safeguard our goals, using an "if-then" model and tackles one of the biggest potential impediments to success—our thoughts. In the next few pages, we will also unpack the difference between reflecting and dwelling and examine the ways in which our self-talk can be based on cognitive distortions.

Using An "If-Then" Framework Can Help You Reach Your Goals

Psychologist Peter M. Gollwitzer, a goal theory researcher, notes that after we set a goal, there is a second step we must take to see our plans materialize. According to Gollwitzer, we are more likely to accomplish goals when we combine them with an "if-then" strategy. An "if-then" plan describes how we will respond to problems that may interfere with our objectives.[43]

Thinking about your law school experience in an "if-then" framework may help you connect specific circumstances ("if I am overwhelmed") with desired outcomes ("then I will ask for help"). I invite you to anticipate potential disruptors that may impede your progress in law school so that you can prepare for them. Think about specific obstacles you may encounter as a law student and brainstorm ways to preemptively minimize their effect on your goals. And if you don't know what you don't know, that's okay too. Here are some common law school sentiments that can help you respond (rather than react) to challenges with awareness and information.

Ask #4: Fill in the blanks below.

- If I am procrastinating, then I will _____.
- If I feel overextended, then I will _____.
- If I want to quit, then I will _____.
- If I don't get the job, scholarship, or call-back interview, then I will _____.

[43] Peter M. Gollwitzer & Paschal Sherran, "Implementation Intentions and Goal Achievement: A Meta-Analysis of Effects and Processes," *Advances in Experimental Social Psychology* 38 (2006) 70.

- If I feel anxious, then I will _____.
- If I feel tired, then I will _____.
- If I don't feel motivated, then I will _____.
- If I can't juggle my academic and personal responsibilities, then I will _____.
- If my personal relationships require more attention, then I will _____.
- If I receive disappointing feedback, then I will _____.

Committing to a goal is one thing but insulating that goal from internal and external distractions is a critical step many fail to take. Not you, though! As a law student, you cannot afford to let external events paralyze you—such as a disappointing exam grade, falling behind in the reading, or a less than stellar interview. Learn from my mistake.

Failing my first law school exam dealt an unexpected blow to my confidence. Seriously, who fails their first open book, pass/fail exam in law school? It felt like my career was over before it started. If I failed my first law school exam, there was no hope of passing the New York bar exam (or so I thought).

Before the first semester of law school officially began, incoming 1Ls were required to take a class called Legal Methods. During this three-week course, the professor previewed foundational legal concepts that we would explore throughout the semester. After the class, we had a four-hour, open-book exam to assess what we had learned.

The way my professor communicated that I had failed the exam was an event in and of itself. It was not a quiet defeat. I didn't get a discrete email with the exam results or have the ability to check the school's online platform to see my grade. Instead, my Legal Methods professor summoned me to her office to break the news in person. Without beating around the bush, she bluntly blurted out, "You failed and will need to retake this exam." If that wasn't enough of a punch in the gut, she continued, "You didn't even answer the questions. You provided the legal standards but didn't respond to the prompts or apply the law to the facts."

Her office transformed into an inferno. I erupted into tears. I was embarrassed and could not catch my breath or slow down my racing heartbeat. This was my first panic attack. I asked the professor if I could be excused to compose myself. In the bathroom, I had one of those uncontrollable, ugly, no, *hideous* cries. After collecting myself as best I could, I walked back into the professor's office and asked her to provide more feedback to better understand next steps.

For the next two years, I rehashed this moment before every exam, before every meeting, before every in-class discussion. I was catastrophizing, always thinking I would clumsily and publicly fall flat on my face. Forecasting failure became a distraction, an extra hurdle I needed to clear before getting my head in the game. This one exam did not predict my future success, but I became fixated on this one moment. After law school, I understood how paralyzing it was to allow my self-worth to fluctuate based on short term events. I tell this story as a cautionary tale of what *not* to do—that is, do not dwell on past disappointments.

Understand The Difference Between Reflecting And Dwelling

There is a difference between *reflecting* and *dwelling*. Reflecting is a healthy, productive exercise where we assess what has occurred and decide how to change our behavior. When we dwell, on the other hand, there's no progress. Nothing changes. It's as if we are stuck in quicksand—the more we struggle in this state of unrest, the deeper we sink into the muck. Dwelling on a perceived setback, like failing your first law school exam, is pointless. We can't go back and change the past. As author John Maxwell reminds us, we should not "relive the things that don't go as planned. This is completely unproductive. Yesterday ended last night."[44] Your perceived failures are not chipping away at you; they are chiseling you into a lawyer who can bounce back from adversity. Ask yourself: How can I grow from this experience?

Dwelling on my first exam failure was a waste of time. I am proof that you can fail your first law school exam and graduate from law school with honors, pass the New York bar exam on the first attempt, clerk on the Sixth Circuit Court of Appeals, work at one of the largest international law firms in the world, and become a published author. And my story is still being written. This is not meant to be a humble brag. It's meant to encourage you to press forward, unrelentingly.

Why do we fixate on negative events? Blame it on the brain, at least partially. Alex Korb explains why we tend to overemphasize negative events:

> [A]ll of our brains—no matter who we are—react more strongly to negative events. Negative events simply seem to carry more weight than positive ones. Losing five dollars makes you more upset than finding five dollars makes you happy. Having a friend tell you you're beautiful doesn't quite balance out the effect of another friend telling you you're ugly.[45]

He calls this effect the "Positivity Ratio" and attributes it to "the asymmetric response to positive and negative events . . . rooted in the brain's processing of emotion."[46] According to Korb:

> All of this means that to be happy in our daily lives, we

---

[44] John Maxwell, *The 15 Invaluable Laws of Growth: Live Them and Reach Your Potential* (Center Street, 2012).

[45] Alex Korb, *The Upward Spiral: Using Neuroscience to Reverse the Course of Depression, One Small Change at a Time*, 50 (New Harbinger Publications, Inc., 2015).

[46] *Id.*

need a high ratio of positive to negative. And it turns out, after considerable study, that ratio is three to one. We need three positive comments from a friend for every negative one, three wins at work for every loss. Everyone's "win ratio" is different. That three-to-one ratio is just an average. Some people might need only a two-to-one ratio and be fine, but others—people who feel losses and disappointments more deeply—might need a higher ratio.[47]

How do we boost our "win ratio"? Create your own opportunities for success. Control the controllables, remember? These individual successes don't have to be monumental, but each one will cumulatively increase your overall win ratio. Attending office hours is one way to proactively create a law school "win." You succeed when a professor confirms that you understand a principle discussed in class. You can also create a "win" by explaining legal concepts to your friends and family to gauge your understanding of a case, increase your retention, and distill difficult fact patterns in preparation for test day. This practice also has the added benefit of allowing you to connect with people in your support system. Rack up wins by volunteering in class, starting your outlines early, and dedicating time to recharge.

Creating a "win" may also involve taking practice exams and getting feedback from professors to confirm that you're on the right track. Reviewing practice tests may reveal aspects of the class that are important to your professor, which can translate into a stronger exam response. Some professors may be willing to review a practice exam with you. Don't pass this up.

When you make a mistake, or when things do not go as planned, how will you course correct? Do you have a "now what" or "recovery" plan at the ready? As you consider these questions, I invite you to think about your thoughts.

[47] *Id.*

Get Your Self-talk Under Control

It all starts with awareness. If we are not attentive to the potentially damaging ways in which we talk to ourselves, we will delay our progress or even quit prematurely. The following cognitive distortions may signal a need to reevaluate our thinking.

- *All or nothing thinking*: Seeing things in black and white without any room for shades of gray. For example, either you are perfect at briefing cases or you are the worst at it.

- *Jumping to conclusions*: Making conclusions and predictions based on inaccurate or incomplete information (e.g., "everyone is studying more than me.") How do you know? You are speculating based on information you do not have.

- *Making "should" or "supposed to" statements*: Projecting what you or others "should do," "ought to do," or "must do."

- *Mental filtering*: Focusing only on negative events and discounting positive ones.

- *Magnification or catastrophizing*: Exaggerating the importance, meaning or significance of events. This is the cognitive distortion I carried with me during law school after failing my first exam.

- *Overgeneralizing*: Identifying one or two examples and convincing yourself that there is a pattern. For example, because one Socratic session did not go well, every time you are called on will be a disaster.

- *Labeling/mislabeling*: Like overgeneralizing, labeling occurs when we assign judgment to events or people based on limited information.

As you read the list of cognitive distortions above, what

patterns of thinking do you gravitate toward? How can you get to the truth?

Sometimes self-talk is deliberately harmful in what it does not say. As an employment lawyer, one of the techniques I use to investigate allegations of workplace misconduct is listening for the gaps. Sometimes what is not said can be just as powerful as what witnesses say during interviews. The same is true when monitoring self-talk. Octavia Raheem, author of *Pause, Rest Be*, encourages us to "[l]isten for what isn't being spoken. You know how fear likes to talk a lot of outrageous smack? What if you got curious about what fear isn't saying? What is fear leaving out of the story that you know is true?"[48]

We must control our thoughts. "Your thoughts are not truths. Your thoughts are not facts. They are simply your thoughts. And you can change your thoughts."[49] Self-talk— our internal monologue—can work for or against us. It can encourage us to make bold moves. But it's just as easy to talk ourselves into a frenzied state of self-doubt. Because we know ourselves better than anyone, we have the best intel into our own weaknesses, vulnerabilities, and insecurities. We have reliable, CIA-level intelligence on ourselves. How dare we become linguistic specialists and use our own words against us! I never thought I was a bully until I started paying attention to the way I spoke to myself. So, I ask, what are you telling yourself as events unfold? How much of what you say leaves you feeling depleted? Why do we use more compassionate language with other people than we do when talking to ourselves? If a so-called "friend" questioned your every move and made you feel inadequate at every turn, you would likely ghost this person.

Guess what? We can *practice* (there's that word again)

---

[48] Octavia Raheem, *Pause, Rest, Be: Stillness Practices for Courage in Times of Change* (Shambhala 2022) 66.
[49] Author unknown.

positive self-talk, especially during stressful periods. If we use our own names to encourage ourselves, rather than the first-person pronoun "I," this can increase our ability to engage in positive self-talk.[50] Using our own name allows us to speak as if we were helping someone else through a difficult time. For example, instead of saying "I deserve to rest," you would use your own name: "Deirdre deserves to rest." How would you encourage your child, a friend, significant other, or mentee who has experienced shame, humiliation, or a perceived setback? Be just as compassionate with yourself and do everything possible to click the "unsubscribe" button when unwanted messages of self-doubt pop into your mental inbox.

Talking Myself Out Of A Panic

Test takers preparing to take the New York State bar examination are given a list of approved items to bring into the examination room. The instructions are so detailed that they even specify what kind of container the items must be placed in: one clear, re-sealable plastic food bag. Here's what I was permitted to bring to the testing facility in 2013.

- Government issued photo ID
- Blue or black ink pens
- Feminine hygiene products
- Quiet snack (unwrapped in clear plastic food storage bag)
- One liter beverage (re-sealable, clear, plastic container stored under the table, labels removed, no glass, cans, or cups)
- Seat ticket (no writing on it at any time)

[50] E. Kross et al., *Self-talk as a Regulatory Mechanism: How You Do it Matters*, J. of Personality & Soc. Psych. 106, 304–24 (2014); I. Grossmann & E. Kross, *Exploring Solomon's Paradox: Self-Distancing Eliminates the Self-Other Asymmetry in Wise Reasoning About Close Relationships in Younger and Older Adults*," PSYCH. SCI. 25, 1571–80 (2014); E. Kross & O. Ayduk, *Self-Distancing: Theory, Research and Current Directions*, Advances in Experimental Soc. Psych. 55, 81–136 (2017).

- No. 2 pencils and erasers
- Medications (in original container)
- Foam earplugs
- Analog wristwatch

On the first day of the bar exam, my "quiet snack" was a delicious cinnamon raisin bagel, lightly toasted with butter. I took one bite, then another. Then the proctor announced, "You may begin the exam," and you could hear every test taker inside the jam-packed New York City Javits Center whip open their exam booklets. As I continued chewing, I felt something loosen in the upper left register of my mouth. At first, I thought it was a raisin that spent a minute too long in the toaster. Continuing to chew, I bit down on something that was harder than any raisin I had ever tasted. Next thing I knew, I was holding my tooth in my hand, seconds into beginning the most important test of my professional career.

No test prep company could have equipped me for this.

In that moment, it was as if two people appeared on each shoulder. You know, like the ones you've seen on TV, representing an angel and a devil. The "devil" bombarded me with a million and one questions. Had I eaten a poisonous bagel? Were more teeth going to fall out? Was this a sign that the law wasn't for me? Should I raise my hand and ask one of the proctors for assistance? Should I silently gather my things and leave the examination room? Am I about to start bleeding all over the place? Do I get a refund on the testing fee? Will my law firm rescind my offer letter if I don't complete this test?

On the other shoulder, appeared the mellow, calm angelic voice, telling me, "Cherelle, you are not in pain. You are safe and not in any danger. Put your tooth in the plastic bag you brought with you, move the tooth bag out of your line of sight, and act like you've got some sense."

There was no way I could do both. I could not panic and take the bar exam simultaneously. I had to decide in that moment whether to proceed or freak out. I chose to put my tooth in my plastic baggie and take the exam.

Thankfully, for the most part, I was able to concentrate on the test. Other than running my tongue over the missing tooth during the exam, I was in the zone and passed the test on the first attempt. Immediately thereafter, I made an appointment with my dentist all to discover that it was my crown (not an actual tooth that had fallen out).

Cross-Examine Your Thoughts

One way to monitor self-talk is to cross-examine the thousands of ideas that pop into our heads daily. The critical, self-destructive voice in our head will only frustrate our ability to shine. Investigating our thoughts allows us to take the perspective of an observer so that we do not automatically believe everything we think. Like many of the techniques in this book, self-questioning requires practice, so be patient as you develop high-quality—not bargain basement—thoughts.

Start honing your cross-examination skills now! In litigation, the purpose of cross-examining a witness is to test the credibility of their statements. This technique can also be used to test the accuracy of our thoughts. Say, for instance, a Socratic session did not go as planned. You can interrogate yourself by asking, "Isn't it true that I did the best I could?," "Isn't it true that I can try again?" "This single event will not make or break my legal career, will it?" "No matter how this turns out, isn't it true that I will be okay?" "I can bounce back from this, right?"

Here's another list of questions that you can ask yourself when you need to interrogate your thoughts:

- Is this thought *true*? When I use the word "true" here, I mean able to be confirmed with concrete, verifiable data, or at least a credible witness.

- Is this thought *helpful*?

- Is this thought *inspiring*?

- Is this thought *necessary*?
- Is this thought *kind*?
- Is that really how it went or just how I (choose to) remember it?
- What if the opposite were true?
- What additional perspectives are needed to confirm or deny the truth of what I'm telling myself?

Closely examining your thoughts is mission critical if you find yourself engaged in the cognitive distortions we discussed earlier. When controversial thoughts arise, give yourself a specific counter-thought that aligns with the evidence. In other words, think like a lawyer! Let's get specific.

Thought: "I'm never going to get ahead with the reading on the syllabus."

Counter-thought: "Although things may seem overwhelming, I am persistent. I am willing to invest the necessary time to read and digest the assigned material. Even if I cannot read every page in excruciating detail, I will use my best judgment and prioritize what I believe to be important. I am not afraid of hard work. I will pace myself."

Thought: "I'm going to fail this exam."

Counter-thought: "I am conscientious and entirely capable of demonstrating all that I have learned this semester. I believe in my ability to figure it out. This is my opportunity to showcase my knowledge. When I sit down to take my exam, I will take deep, full breaths and trust that what I have studied has adequately prepared me to do my best."

Thought: "I'm not cut out for this."

Counter-thought: "I am doing my best and am not afraid to ask for help when I need it. I know I can do this because I'm resourceful and have already accomplished so much. I have the mental, physical, and emotional stamina to do this work."

Thought: "There's no way I'm going to get a job with these grades."

Counter-thought: "I have so much to contribute, and I shine in unique ways. When I get the opportunity to speak about my accomplishments during an interview, I will do so proudly, knowing that I can perform with excellence. No one can take my place."

> *The most powerful words in the universe*
> *are the words you say to yourself.*
>
> —Marie Forleo

Talk About What You Are Feeling

In addition to cross-examining your thoughts, you may need to vent to someone who has earned your trust. Selectively choose your confidant. This person can be a classmate, who understands first-hand the demands of law school, or someone outside your law school community. Your non-lawyer friends and family may not be able to help you understand the "rule against perpetuity," but they can still hold space for you. Use the tools from chapter 3 to help communicate what you need to feel supported. If the negative thoughts become overwhelming or start to impact your mental health, use the resources available on campus to get help.

Based on the thousands of thoughts we have each day, some of them will be duds. Some of our thoughts pass by without much attention, others have more stickiness. I invite you to think about your thoughts as an exercise of self-compassion. You now have tools to monitor self-talk, listen for what you may *not* be saying to yourself, recognize cognitive distortions, and cross-examine yourself based on what you know to be true.

Solo Sidebar

1. How can you hold yourself lovingly accountable when you fall short of your expectations?

2. What are rock-solid truths that you know about your-

self and your abilities? In other words, what do you know for certain about who you are? These bedrock truths can help you use evidence-backed responses to confront negative self-talk.

3. How can you accumulate law school wins?

4. When you reflect on a challenging week in law school, what can you be proud of? How can you remind yourself that you did your absolute best?

Concluding Mindfulness Practice: Seated Inversion

Inversions can improve circulation and improve lymphatic drainage, leading us to feel more energized and less sluggish. When I hear the word "inversion" in yoga, I envision someone in a headstand, handstand, or shoulder stand, effortlessly balancing on the forearms or hands. If you are like me and get immediately intimidated by these images, there's no need to get bent out of shape. An inversion can be as simple as a forward fold (imagine bending over your legs to tie your shoes or downward-facing dog, creating an upside-down V-shape with your body). An inversion simply means that your head is positioned below your heart.

For this seated inversion, plant the soles of your feet on the floor. Separate your knees so that when you lean forward, your torso has a clear path to travel toward the ground. Elongate the spine and slowly hinge forward from your hips, and let your chest melt toward the floor. In this forward fold, nod your head "yes" and "no" to release tension in your neck. Take a few full breaths in this position and, when you are ready, slowly roll up to the original seated position. If you lift your head too quickly, it may make you feel dizzy or lightheaded. So, please take your time coming back to a neutral stance. I love seated inversions because they are accessible to everyone—all you need is a comfortable seat and the willingness to try.

8

BE INTENTIONAL WITH YOUR TIME

Multitasking is the wellspring of office gaffes, as well as the stock answer to how we do more with less when in fact we're usually doing less with more. What now passes for multitasking was once called not paying attention.

—Jared Sandberg

Call it what you want. Some describe our chronic distraction as "multitasking." Others say it's "doing more with less." I get a kick out of this definitionn of multitasking: "screwing up several things at once."[51]

However we define multitasking, the truth is, every day we are bombarded with innumerable tasks and responsibilities competing for our full attention. This forces us to decide, whether consciously or subconsciously, what and who deserves our time. Despite the dizzying methods to "connect" at our disposal, we are more detached from the relationships and activities we claim to cherish. With so much vying for the spotlight, multitasking is the only way to see results, right? Researchers disagree.

Multitasking Decreases Our Productivity

Does multitasking increase our productivity? Do we actually accomplish more when simultaneously juggling different activities? Do we value the illusion of productivity simply because we are busy? We know what multitasking looks like—whether it's reading with the TV on, scrolling mindlessly on social media while attempting to work, or texting someone while a loved one talks about their day.

[51] Author unknown.

Research shows that multitasking does *not* make us more productive because our brains are not wired to perform several tasks at once. The etymology of the term "multitask" originated from the idea that computers could perform multiple tasks simultaneously. This concept was later applied to people, but in reality, when we think we are multitasking, we are actually switch-tasking. Earl Miller, a neuroscientist at the Massachusetts Institute of Technology, notes that our brains are "not wired to multitask well... When people think they're multitasking, they're actually just switching from one task to another very rapidly. And every time they do, there's a cognitive cost in doing so."[52] In one study, employees took 25 minutes to recover from distractions like emails and phone calls before they could return to their original assignment.[53] That time adds up.

When distractions arise, the brain has a choice—it can (1) ignore the distraction and remain focused on the present task or (2) entertain the diversion and return to the initial project later on. Do we select option one or two? Making this threshold decision takes time away from the initial assignment. With switch-tasking, our brain must re-familiarize itself with the primary and secondary task each time we move through the stop-and-go process. This inevitably increases the time needed to complete a single project.[54] And the more time we spend on tasks, the more exhausted we may feel because of multitasking.

In fact, there's a reason we may feel depleted when multitasking. Alternating between tasks consumes glucose, the

[52] Damien Massias, *The Magpie Effect: Your Complete and Comprehensive Guide to Surviving and Enjoying the Twisted Social Media Era*, Matador, at 161 (2019).

[53] Gloria Mark, *The Cost of Interrupted Work: More Speed and Stress*, https://www.ics.uci.edu/~gmark/chi08-mark.pdf.

[54] Claudia Wallis, *The Multitasking Generation*, TIME, Mar. 27, 2006, http://www.balcells.com/blog/images/articles/entry558_2465_multi-tasking.pdf.

energy needed to power our brain cells. In addition, multi-tasking can release the stress hormones cortisol and adrenaline, which power our fight, flight, or freeze responses. If constantly activated, these hormones can negatively impact our health. As a law student, when it's time to review the Federal Rules of Civil Procedure or begin outlining for final exams, your body and mind should be receptive to processing new information and not in fight-or-flight mode. You do not want stress hormones activated while attempting to absorb complex material. It is much harder to access your creativity and problem-solving skills in this state.

Multitasking Makes Our Work Less Accurate

Our work is less accurate when we perform more than one task at a time. Picture this: You are sitting in contracts class, diligently taking notes, and listening to your professor discuss the elements of promissory estoppel.[55] An email notification pops up, and you respond, assuring yourself that it will only take a quick moment to reply to the email. You tell yourself you can do both tasks without missing a beat. Maybe you *think* you can. But seemingly small detours and distractions add up, and they may create behavioral patterns that become habits. Somewhere along the line, you may overlook an important detail that your professor mentions in class and that shows up on the final exam.

Multitasking Impacts How We Process Information

Multitasking changes the way we learn, process, and retain information. Neurophysiologists suggest that superficial learning occurs when we multitask. In other words, learning while multitasking has a "different cognitive status than that of uninterrupted learning, and is actually less efficient and useful than uninterrupted learning."[56] Learning occurs in

---

[55] Promissory estoppel is a principle that allows a party to recover damages if the party reasonably relied on a promise to their detriment.
[56] Charles J. Abaté, *You Say Multitasking Like It's a Good Thing,* Thought

two distinct areas of the brain—the hippocampus and the striatum. Each area implicates a specific type (and quality) of learning. When we concentrate on one task at a time, we engage in declarative learning, which takes place in the hippocampus. Declarative learning allows us to retain information and apply it to new facts. The newly acquired information is also better organized and easier to manipulate.

On the other hand, when we multitask, habitual learning takes place in the brain's striatum and "results in learning that is automatic, almost subconscious, but much more limited in its applicability to new situations."[57] Here's the bottom line: complete one task with deliberateness and give your brain a chance to properly retain information. It's that simple (notice, I didn't say "easy").

Multitasking is a choice. We can decide whether to frantically shuffle between different tasks or approach each project with deep-focused thinking. How can you show up to your work, your to-do lists, with an attitude of ease? This does not mean pretending that things are easy when they are not. You already know how I feel about toxic positivity.

Approach the tasks at hand with a lightness, an openness, an unshakable expectancy that, no matter what, you can relax into and through the project.

A few years into practicing law, I started implementing a radical idea to handle the urge to multitask. On days when my inbox was bursting at the seams with "high importance" requests and the phone was constantly ringing, I simply stopped. I moved more slowly. More intentionally. I ate and drank something nourishing, instead of chugging another cup of coffee. I listened to what my needs were in those moments. I resolved to focus on one thing at a time. I took breaks between tasks. I planted my feet. I took luxurious breath breaks. I loosened my grip. I massaged my jaw.

& Action, v. 24 (National Education Ass'n Fall 2008).
[57] *Id.*

When I approach things with a sense of ease, I start with a relaxed body. I noticed where the tension was lurking—my jaw, shoulders, back and put my hand on that area and release it. I'll admit, I know from experience what it feels like to do it the opposite way—frantically shifting from one thing to another. But this no longer works for me—it makes me leak energy, *and* it does not increase my productivity.

Single-tasking may require you to change certain behaviors. During class, you may have to take notes by hand or turn your Wi-Fi off to avoid being distracted by email or the latest "breaking news" alert. You may need to put your cell phone away or turn it off so you don't see text messages or social media notifications pop up.

Juggling different projects at once prevents you from truly engaging with others and being tuned into the task in front of you. It's more difficult to connect when multitasking. If you resist multitasking now, you will develop positive habits when you have even more demands on your time and energy as a lawyer. Be disciplined. Do one thing at a time. Do it with excellence. Do it with thoughtfulness and care.

Spend More Time Deeply Working and Deeply Resting

We have spent the last several pages talking about the importance of being deliberate with your attention when you sit down to study. Your breaks and periods of rest should be approached with the same level of intentionality. As a law student you can develop smart habits around savoring your free time. If you are going to run on the treadmill for an hour, be entirely on the treadmill for that hour without reading and responding to emails. In other words, take whole-hearted breaks. I challenge you to be intentional with how you spend your time, whether that means engaging in deep work or deep rest.

Solo Sidebar

1. Name three distractions or habits that make it chal-

lenging to focus on one task at a time. What is the easiest next step you can take to minimize these distractions?

2. What ritual(s) or routine(s) help you transition into a focused work state?

3. How can you create a study environment that limits distractions?

In his popular TedTalk on languishing, organizational psychologist Adam Grant, notes that on average, people check emails seventy-four times a day. He describes a phenomenon where people shred what could be meaningful periods of time into tiny useless moments. Referring to this as "time confetti," Grant calls dividing our time in this way as "enemy of energy and excellence." Rather than multitask, where do you have time at the margins to engage in deep work or rest? For example, maybe it's twenty minutes before your next class is scheduled to start. How can you use these seemingly insignificant pockets of time productively? Note that sometimes, the most productive thing you can do is take a nap.

Concluding Mindfulness Practice: Linking Breath to Movement

This is another practice that activates the connection between breath and movement. Find a comfortable position seated or standing. Begin with an engaged core and tall spine. Inhale, lift your arms up and over your head as if you are painting the walls with your fingertips. As you inhale, allow your chest to expand, creating spaciousness across your shoulders. Complete the inhale by bringing the palms together to touch over your head. On an exhale, lower the arms down to your side. Repeat this sequence as many times as you desire.

9

Boldly Resist Mediocrity

Mediocrity will never do. You are capable of something better.
—Gordon B. Hinckley

In dance, there is a difference between "marking" choreography and performing a routine "full out." Before law school, I danced professionally with a repertory theater company in Philadelphia, called Freedom Theatre, cofounded by the late John E. Allen Jr. and Robert Leslie. I remember one dress rehearsal with the ensemble before opening night. Our choreographer wanted the dancers to perform the entire combination from start to finish, anxious to see how the music, lights, costumes, and blocking would look on stage. The choreographer rhythmically cued in the dancers to begin—"five, six, seven, eight"—in unison with the music. The dancers began moving, but some of them "marked" the routine, replacing intense leaps with miniature hops or hand gestures to pantomime the actual movements. Instead of turning on relevé (on their toes), the dancers mimicked the actual turns by twirling an index finger to indicate the number of times they were supposed to revolve. Those who marked the combination were holding back the emotion, depth, and fervor associated with performance-quality movement. Maybe they were trying to conserve energy for opening night. Whatever the reason for this non-committal demonstration, the choreographer was irritated.

"Stop the music, lights up," she abruptly demanded, as if the dancers had intentionally disrespected her creative life's work. "Cue everything from the top. I want to see the combination again, this time full out, please." We knew exactly what she meant by "full out," but in case anyone was confused, the choreographer continued, "No one will pay money to see you half-perform this piece. When you mark the choreography, your body won't know what it's like to give it your all. If this is the way you practice, this is the way you will perform during the show. Now isn't the time to mark it. Start again, this time, do it full out."

Some students meander through law school by "marking" the experience. They are on autopilot, going through the motions, substituting depth for the shallow, whispering (or remaining silent) when they should shout, camouflaging when they should stand out, shrinking when their power lies in expanding. Law school, like choreography, should not be marked.

Stealthily flying under the radar in law school and doing the bare minimum to "get by" is a missed opportunity. You have too much to contribute to the legal profession to be content with mediocrity. Although your comfort zone may shield you from potential embarrassment, nothing groundbreaking occurs there. It's basic and boring.

I don't want you to settle in law school. I want you to make being uncomfortable a habit. Not many of us would challenge ourselves to wake up in the morning and ask, "So, how can I make myself uncomfortable today?" What would happen if we started asking this question? How would this change our perspective and actions?

So, how do 1Ls "settle" in law school? Students settle by not reviewing practice exams with their professors, believing they will get a B or B- no matter what because of the grading curve. During 1L year, most students are expected to get Bs as the median grade, with a few students falling above and below this point. Students settle when they refuse to attend office hours because certain professors appear unapproachable. Students settle when they sense discomfort and disengage, convincing themselves that, if they play it safe, they will avoid mistakes. Now that you know what settling in law school can look like, the remainder of this chapter offers suggestions on how you can soar above the mediocre.

"Study to Become the Lawyer You Would Want to Hire."

One of my pre-law professors at Boston University offered students a thoughtful perspective on how to avoid a lackluster attitude in law school. He encouraged us to "study to become the lawyer you would want to hire." I love this advice because it applies to every profession. If you are studying to be a structural engineer, be willing to drive your car across the bridge you designed. If you are a website designer, would you be comfortable entering your credit card information or social security number on the website you created? If you are studying to become a psychiatrist, be the type of doctor you would see yourself. The practicality of this advice extends to our relationships too. We should aim to be the partner we would want to marry; the child we would want to have; the sibling we would support unconditionally; the selfless friend we would want by our side.

No one wants to pay for average, certainly not when the stakes are high. Soon, you will be paid to assist individuals and corporations with the problems that keep them up at night. The multi-million-dollar deal, the impact litigation that will determine the rights and civil liberties of generations to come, the jury trial that stands to provide closure and justice to victims or set an innocent person free. None of these clients want average, and neither would you.

Lawyers Are Oath Takers

If you find yourself falling into the lull of mediocrity, remember that lawyers must take an "Oath of Admission" before becoming a licensed attorney. After graduating from law school and passing the bar, there's one final step before you can add "Esq." after your name—your swearing in ceremony. Each state has its own oath, but each contains an obligation to uphold the federal Constitution and the state constitution in the jurisdiction in which you will practice. The New York oath states as follows:

> I do solemnly swear (or affirm) that I will support the constitution of the United States, and the constitution of the State of New York, and that I will faithfully discharge the duties of the office of attorney and counselor-at-law, according to the best of my ability.

When I raised my right hand to say the New York oath, I was holding space for multiple emotions: pride from surviving three laborious years of law school, confusion over how I had amassed nearly $200,000 of debt in such a short period of time, gratitude for passing the New York bar exam, and excitement about finally starting my legal career. This oath signaled a responsibility, a weightiness, a seriousness associated with the work ahead. The Oath of Admission is a rite of passage that transforms you from an ordinary citizen to an officer of the court. Lawyers are among the few professions where an oath is *required* by statute before you can obtain a license to practice. If you know the state where you intend to be licensed, read the oath you will take one day, decide what those promises mean to you, and consider making additional vows to yourself about how you will show up as a law student.

The Time To ~~Network~~ Connect Is Now

Minimize mediocrity in law school by treating the experience like a three-year connecting event. I am intentionally not using the word networking here. For me, the word has an opportunist connotation, and as an introvert, whenever I hear that word, I immediately start planning my escape from the event. But let's reframe the term networking and distill it to its essence: connection and curiosity. When you interact with other people, go beyond the superficial. Share stories, aspirations, moments of frustration, disappointment, and elation. You don't know where your classmates will end up personally or professionally. Get to know the people around you. Down the line, a former classmate could be your client, business partner in a startup venture, best friend, or spouse. My point is, the right connection can transform your life.

Engage With Your Professors

You are not just passing through law school. You are there to show up *and* shine, remember? Part of your mission is to get to know your professors. Even the instructor with a permanent scowl can be an ally or mentor. No matter what, make your office hours debut within the first few weeks of the first semester. If you feel uncomfortable visiting professors by yourself, go with other students. This is another chance to bond with your classmates and create moments that you will remember years after law school.

Imagine the opportunity to visit Barack Obama, Elizabeth Warren, Elena Kagan, and other former professors who shared their brilliance in the classroom. Unfortunately, many students do not maximize opportunities to interact with professors outside of the classroom, and this is as important as preparing for class and final exams. Bona fide connections are made *before* you need someone to act on your behalf. When you need an introduction or letters of recommendation, your relationship seeds should already be planted, germinated, and show signs of growth. The most compelling letters of recommendation convey a personal connection, a genuine relationship with the person who vouches for you. This cannot happen if you are simply a name on a seating chart that gets shredded at the end of the semester and forgotten after grades are posted. The goal is to have *at least one* professor who remembers your name 20 years after you graduate from law school.

Early in the semester, you may not have specific questions about the course material, and that's okay. There may be times when you don't know what you don't know. Instead of attending office hours with nothing to ask, here are a few starter questions to keep in mind: How does this case fit into the larger theory of contract law? How does it build on the reading from the previous weeks? How do you annotate a case as you read?

Your first visit can be an introductory meeting to learn about the professor's background and career trajectory. Read their biographies and ask questions about their research, articles they are writing, what pro bono projects motivate them, and how they stay informed about developments in their respective fields. In other words, get curious about the person teaching you. Ask your professors to recommend resources to supplement the assigned reading. Explore the impact of current events on the various doctrines you are studying. Seek writing opportunities and input on any written work you have done. The more you interact with professors during the semester, the more confidence you will develop before exam day.

As the semester progresses, office hours also provide an alternative way to participate in a course, without the pressure of the Socratic method. In a more relaxed environment, you can engage on your own terms without "performing" in front of your peers. These one-on-one discussions have the added benefit of making in-class conversations more intriguing because you are interacting with the material in a personal way.

After your first semester, review *all* of your exams with your professors. This is the simplest and most effective way to improve your exam-taking skills. Please prioritize this. Most professors do not automatically return graded exams to their students. Those who do, typically provide minimal written comments, if any. To get the most value from your exam, schedule time with your professor to compare your responses to the "model answer." Did you spot each legal issue? Which ones did you miss? How can you avoid this on future exams? Did you identify the correct legal principle(s) to analyze? Did you discuss irrelevant facts? Was your analysis as detailed as the model answer? How was the model answer structured? Was your writing crisp? Even if you received all the "points" for a specific issue, ask the professor to review your response anyway. If you systematically do this with each professor, you may notice patterns in the way you take exams and discover ways to improve. For example, some classes in law school are heavily rules or statute-based. And you may recognize strategies that can be applied to other rules-based classes such as the Federal Rules of Civil Procedure, the Federal Rules of Evidence, the Bankruptcy Code, and tax laws.

No matter the grade you received, set your ego aside and ask for feedback on improving your legal analysis and writing. You may not be able to change your grade (that's not the goal anyway), but you will enhance your performance on future exams.

Take A Genuine Interest In Your Classmates

Your law school experience and entire career will be enhanced by getting to know your fellow students. If your law school offers mentorship programs that pair 1Ls with more senior classmates, please consider participating. You may be thinking, "I don't have problems making friends—why do I need a formal mentorship program to meet people?" Structured programs can be advantageous because 2Ls and 3Ls may not live on campus and sometimes their schedules allow for more time outside of the classroom to participate in extracurriculars. If upperclassmen already have a job lined up post-graduation, they may be uninterested in spending more time than necessary on campus. But they are in the best possible position to empathize with you. Not only have they survived the unique challenges of 1L year, but they are also close enough to the experience that they will vividly remember how they made it through the most difficult year of law school. Often, their intel goes beyond what's on the law school's website or in the glossy orientation materials. They can give you the scoop on professors, exams, what courses to take, clinics, rewarding extracurriculars, publicized and unpublicized resources on and off campus, including off-the-beaten-path places to study and eat.

2Ls and 3Ls will also have their pulse on the legal market, and most will be willing to share insights regarding hiring processes. These students are underutilized resources.

Are you ready for this secret—it's something career services will not tell you. Years down the line, some of your classmates may be in positions of influence to hire you.

After law school, I assisted one of my supervisors preliminarily review resumes for new hires. While pouring over the resumes and cover letters we received, I immediately recognized a former classmate's name at the top of the page. We graduated the same year and had taken several classes together. When the time came to provide feedback on my experiences with this person, I was honest. Let me put it this way, if this person knew I was the gatekeeper, in a position to advance his resume, he would have carried himself differently when we were in class together.

Think Expansively As It Relates To Your Career

When considering how to use your law degree, remind yourself that your post graduate options are not limited to what career services shares. When I considered life after law school, it felt like there were only two viable options: public interest or private practice at a law firm. But there's more—legal compliance, working for any company in a legal capacity (referred to as working "in-house"), politics, lobbying, academia, public policy, entrepreneurship—the list truly is endless. Don't take my word for it. Talk to alumni who can provide insight into paths they have taken.

I know law school is expensive and some students (myself included) felt compelled to work for a law firm to repay the mounds of debt I had ~~accrued~~, I mean invested. Even if you take a job so that you can pay your student loans, there is more, if you so desire.

You Can Be A Lawyer…And

Let's also not forget about the people who practice law *and* excel in other fulfilling areas. It's possible!

- Linda Rose (lawyer/jazz musician). "I am an organizer," she says. "I have my own law firm, and I approached organizing a band the same way."[58] Today, Rose on Vibes plays at least once per month and has played up to six times per month.

- Todd Graves (lawyer/rancher). Todd has always appreciated his ability to pursue dual careers. "I couldn't practice law if I didn't have this other interest," he says. "I am just not bookish enough to do only that; I got to have something on the side."[59]

- Nina Lacher (lawyer/fashion blogger). Florida civil litigator Nina Lacher cares about what she wears, and that led her to a second career as a fashion blogger.[60]

- Grace Burrowes (lawyer/writer). New York Times best-selling romance novelist Grace Burrowes has always been a writer, but she came late to publishing. Novel writing, she says, is something lawyers are well-suited to do. "We love words, we have grist for the favorite mills, and we are good with deadlines and contracts," she says, adding that "creative

[58] Jenny B. Davis, "These Lawyers Balance Full-Time Practices with a Side Hustle That Pays." *ABA Journal,* 1 May 2018, www.abajournal.com/magazine/article/side_hustle_lawyers_side_projects/P1.
[59] *Id.*
[60] *Id.*

self-expression is good for us."

Hold on to the activities and interests that make you feel whole. Just because you are studying law does not mean you must say goodbye to soap sculpting (yes, that is a thing).

As you work to transcend mediocrity in your engagement with law school, your peers, professors, and alumni, push yourself to take risky, colossal leaps. And remember, stick to the things within your control.

- Design your own law school course (yes, this is possible).

- Volunteer to conduct research with a professor you admire.

- Ask that nerdy hot student on a date. Why not leave law school with a JD and a life partner? That's *really* getting your money's worth.

Have fun experimenting and playing. Transcending mediocrity is not about comparing yourself to anyone else. It's about asking what more *you* can do and focusing on how *you* can improve. When you reach beyond mediocrity, you will have peace of mind, knowing that you gave it your all. No regrets, remember?

Ask #5: Re-read your law school personal statement.

If you experience a law school lull, try re-reading your law school personal statement. Reminders are powerful ways to maintain focus and increase motivation. Sometimes we need to be reminded of why we started, where we are going and why the destination is important to us. Re-reading your personal statement may give you just the boost you need to transcend mediocrity.

What did you share with the admissions committee in your personal statement? Did you write about what inspires and excites you? What you care about? What issues aggravate you? What you want your legacy to be? Where do you

dream about dedicating your efforts? Maybe you've already
answered some of these questions. If not, perhaps being ex-
posed to new ideas and people have jumpstarted an interest
in an area of law you have never considered. It's okay if
what you wrote about in your law school personal statement
has changed altogether or morphed into some other interest.

The things that excite you are not random.
They are connected to your purpose. Follow them.

—Terrie Davoll Hudson

Ignite Your Pro Bono Practice During Law School

Pro bono work is a great way to sidestep mediocrity because
it requires a shift in perspective. Pro bono work is invigorating, soul work. It is also an act of self-care. If you are
scratching your head asking, "how can I take care of myself
by taking care of someone else" or "won't pro bono work
just add another thing to my already demanding schedule?"
As counterintuitive as it may seem, helping other people will
facilitate your wellness journey in law school and as a practicing attorney. The late Justice Ruth Bader Ginsburg stated
that "a lawyer will gain large satisfaction when he or she is
not simply a fee-charging artisan, but a contributor to the
public good."

Participating in pro bono as a law student shakes up the
monotony of classes, increases connectivity and gives you
purpose. It spices things up and offers meaningful legal work
now. For example, after the malaise of spending all week attending lectures and the balance of your free time studying
in the library, it is energizing to meet with real clients with
real needs. This is a wonderful reminder that what you are
learning goes beyond the classroom.

The legal profession is built on helping others. The American Bar Association urges all attorneys "regardless of professional prominence or professional workload" to perform
a minimum of fifty hours of pro bono services annually to

those unable to pay. Each state can modify this recommended number of pro bono hours. New York has gone a step further by requiring all JD and LLM graduates to complete fifty hours of law related pro bono work before they are admitted to the New York Bar. *See* 22 NYCRR 520.16. No matter how you decide to use your law degree, remember that lawyers have an obligation to serve.

Start Serving Clients In Law School

It is never too early to dive into pro bono work. Yes, even as a law student. Many law schools offer pro bono opportunities for students to get hands on experience practicing their craft and making a difference in someone's life.

My first pro bono experience involved working as a courtroom advocate with Sanctuary for Families' Center for Battered Women's Legal Services. Licensed attorneys supervised law students as they assisted domestic violence survivors seeking protective orders in New York City's family courts. Students helped these survivors draft petitions for protective orders, advocate for them at their initial appearance before Family Court judges, educate them about the Family Court process, and provide safety planning and referrals.

This was the first time I sat across the table, looking at someone eye-to-eye who was entrusting me with her safety. My client expected something from me. She exhausted all other options. This was the first time I felt like a lawyer. And this taste of advocacy reminded me to continue studying to be the lawyer I would want to hire.

Pro bono work will benefit not only the individuals and organizations you will serve, but it will also have profound professional advantages. For example, pro bono work can:

- Create potentially long-lasting relationships with practicing lawyers, clients, and students from other law schools.

- Expose you to areas of law that you had not considered pursuing. Your heart could have been set on becoming a tax lawyer, but one meaningful pro bono immigration project may change the course of your career.

- Help broaden your perspective by thinking about the needs of others.

- Energize and remind you that you are representing real people in the real world with real problems.

- Contextualize the doctrines and legal theories you study in class.

- Give you practical, legal skills to put on your resume at an early stage of your career.

There is a treasure trove of pro bono projects to participate in as a law student and not all of them require long-term commitments. They can be semester long endeavors or short-term assignments like learning about a subject matter during a workshop and then staffing a hotline or interviewing clients for intake purposes. Other opportunities include the following:

- Representing low-income litigants on family law matters, including custody issues, domestic violence reports, and orders of protection;

- Protecting the rights of employees who have been unlawfully terminated or denied unemployment benefits;

- Developing environmental law and policy and promoting environmental justice

- Assisting clients with tax filings and improving financial literacy;

- Ensuring access to healthcare, including reproductive rights;

- Exonerating individuals who have been wrongfully

convicted of a crime;

- Promoting domestic and international human rights;

- Providing legal services to individuals seeking to secure or adjust their immigration status in the United States, including policy research projects;

- Representing tenants in housing court and assisting them secure affordable housing;

- Offering legal services to individuals who are experiencing homelessness or are housing insecure;

- Advocating for students facing suspension and other disciplinary measures;

- Promoting the rights of trans and non-binary people;

- Protecting the interests of animals through the legal system;

- Advocating for the rights of seniors in connection with housing, employment, and health care, including protection against elder abuse, neglect, and fraud.

Some charitable organizations may rely on law students to assist with internal governance and organizational issues. Your school may even offer spring break, winter break or summer opportunities to perform pro bono work domestically and internationally (some schools even fund the trip). As the list above shows, the opportunities for pro bono while in law school are limitless.

At the end of the day, mediocrity does not advance movements. It's not strategic, engaging, or disruptive. Mediocrity does not create change. It fuels regret. You do not want to look back on your law school experience wishing you had gone to office hours, joined a study group, or participated in a clinic to gain practical skills. Fight against complacency with all you have. Settling can be tempting, but it doesn't benefit anyone, especially when you are meant to shine bright.

Solo Sidebar

1. What would a fully engaged, locked-in, on the edge of your seat, law school experience look like?

2. Write your personal law school oath. What vows can you make to yourself in this oath? After you've written down your personal oath, refer to it as the semester progresses to ensure that your actions are aligning with your values.

3. How can you personalize the challenge to transcend mediocrity? In what ways are you willing to step outside of your comfort zone and create opportunities to shine?

Concluding Mindfulness Practice: Neck Rolls

Find a comfortable seated or standing position and engage your core as you lengthen your spine. Drop your chin to your chest. Roll your head to the right, bringing your right ear to your right shoulder. As the head rolls to the back, exposing the front of the throat, be careful not to drop your head too forcefully on the seven small bones that comprise the cervical spine at the base of your neck. Continue the circle by allowing your left ear to meet your left shoulder before lifting your head up and back to a neutral starting point. Repeat this exercise, starting in the opposite direction.

CONCLUSION

Enthusiasm is one of the most powerful engines of success. When you do a thing, do it with all of your might. Put your whole soul into it. Stamp it with your own personality. Be active, be energetic and faithful, and you will accomplish your objective. Nothing great was ever achieved without enthusiasm.

—Ralph Waldo Emerson

It may not seem like it today, but graduation is right around the corner. So, roll up your sleeves and create moments of significance. Moments you will be proud of. To do this, think about ideas you want to explore and projects you want to execute. How will you impact those you encounter over the next three years? How will you contribute to your law school community? How will you act in ways that will outlast your three years in law school? Will you make a commitment to engage in activities that electrify you? Will you be intentional about experimenting with the unfamiliar?

When you walk across the stage at graduation, I don't want you to regret any aspect of your three-year adventure. To make this your reality, refuse to let fear dictate your decisions.

By moving forward despite the fear, you can better determine when to shout "yes!" to opportunities. Say yes even if the outcome is unknown, even if you feel unprepared or unqualified (trust me, you will figure it out). Apply for a clerkship even if you don't think you have "clerkship grades." Go after the dream job even if your academic record is average. Raise your hand in class even if you have not completely formulated the question or answer. Take a genuine interest in your classmates even if that sometimes means, occasionally, cutting your library time short.

When you envision yourself saying "yes," does the activity make you feel expansive or constricted? Octavia Raheem puts it this way: "The quality of your yes matters." Can you complete the task with some pizzazz? With whole heartedness? With gravitas? Is there some horsepower behind your yes? Just because an extracurricular activity may look good on your resume doesn't mean you should pursue it. Ask yourself:

- Does this activity or job matter to me?
- Does this activity or job make a difference?
- Does it align with my calling?
- If I say yes, who will it benefit?
- Am I doing it because it sounds enjoyable?
- Is this consistent with the lifestyle I want to have?
- If money were irrelevant, would I still invest time and energy into the activity?

If you're not saying "HELL YEAH!" about doing something say "no." When deciding whether to do something, if you feel anything less than "Wow! That would be amazing! Absolutely! Hell yeah!—then say "no."

—Derek Sivers

Monitoring the quality of your yes will help prevent over-committing and keep you aligned with your purpose. It's a reliable test to assess our motivation. At the end of the day, you are fashioning a life, not checking off boxes of activities that you "should" participate in. Says who? You are best positioned to know, more than anyone else, the projects that give you a surge of electricity. Sometimes we can go with the flow so much that we forget we have a say in the matter.

The final litmus test to help you gauge the quality of your "yes" comes from *The Almanack of Naval Ravikant*. "If you can't decide, the answer is no. If faced with a difficult choice, such as: Should I marry this person? Should I take this job?

Should I buy this house? Should I move to this city? Should I go into business with this person? If you cannot decide, the answer is no. And the reason is, modern society is full of options. There are tons and tons of options. We live on a planet of seven billion people, and we are connected to everybody on the internet. There are hundreds of thousands of careers available to you. There are so many choices."[61]

As you begin the life-changing experience of law school, show up knowing your worth. Shine in law school by taking risks, by being endlessly curious, by sharing your opinions, by being bold and unapologetic. Shine in law school by thinking and acting mighty. You are ready for this.

---

[61] Eric Jorgenson, *The Almanack of Naval Ravikant* (Magrathea Publishing, 2020) 111.